The HOLY TRINITY
and US

The HOLY TRINITY and US

Viewing the Holy Trinity from Practical Theology Perspective

Prof John Gatungu Githiga

The Regency Publishers

Copyright © 2022 by Prof John Gatungu Githiga.

All rights reserved. No part of this book may be reproduced in any form or by any electronic or mechanical means, including information storage and retrieval systems, without permission in writing from the author and publisher, except by reviewers, who may quote brief passages in a review.

Library of Congress Control Number: 2022917363

ISBN: 978-1-959434-04-7 (Paperback Edition)
ISBN: 978-1-959434-05-4 (Hardcover Edition)
ISBN: 978-1-959434-03-0 (E-book Edition)

Book Ordering Information

The Regency Publishers, US
521 5th Ave 17th floor NY, NY10175
Phone Number: (315)537-3088 ext 1007
Email: info@theregencypublishers.com
www.theregencypublishers.com

Printed in the United States of America

Contents

Acknowledgement iii

Introduction v

Chapter One The Holy Trinity And Victory 1

Chapter Two The Holy Trinity And Provision 3

Chapter Three The Holy Trinity And Transfiguration 7

Chapter Four The Holy Trinity And Holiness 10

Chapter Five Holy Trinity Tranforms Through Fire 18

Chapter Six The Holy Trinity Heals Superiority And Infriority Complex 20

Chapter Seven Holy Trinity And Supernatural Protection 26

Chapter Eight Holy Trinity And Victory Over Persecution 29

Chapter Nine The Holy Trinity And Mission To The Gentile 33

Chapter Ten The Holy Trinity And Blessing 36

Chapter Eleven The Holy Trinity And Baptism Of Jesus ... 39

Chapter Twelve Holy Trinity And Doubt 43

Chapter Thirteen The Holy Trinity Is Irsistable Light 45

Chapter Fourteen Holy Trinity And Greatcommission 47

Chapter Fifteen The Trinity And Good Samaritan.............49

Chapter Sixteen The Holy Trinity And Transformation 51

Chapter Seventeen The Holy Trinity And African Psychology...57

Chapter Eighteen The Tree Of God And Pastoral Care......69

Chapter Nineteen The Great Father And Pastral Care 72

Chapter Twenty The Great Mother And Pastoral Care.......75

Chapter Twenty One The Sermon On The Holy Trinity....77

Chapter Twenty Two Athanasian Creed............................82

ACKNOWLEDGEMENT

I am most grateful to Dr David Brister and Mr. Todd E. -Tazner for proofreading this book and Rev Dr. Mary Githiga for being the most faithful companion and helper.

INTRODUCTION

God has been persistently asking me to write on the Holy Trinity, but I have been having fear of writing about the mystery of a God who has revealed himself as one in three. But God has asked me profound questions about myself. John, do you have three doctorates- Doctorate of Ministry, Doctorate of Religious Education, and a Doctorate of Divinity? Do those three doctorates belong to one person? Do they live in harmony?

Think about the people who participated in your wedding: Were they not from three African nations-Kikuyu, Lou and Luya, and three European nations- Australian bishop was a celebrant, A British Lady provided you with the wedding cake, and a Scottish presbyterian with a honey moon mansion? Were there not three Church Army Captains- Solomon Ng'ang'a your best man, Captain Habel your brother, and Captain John Gatungu? Were there not three flower girls, and yet this was one wedding?

How about your golden wedding anniversary? Were there not three nations, Kenyan, Russian American who was your best man and Irish American who was the maid of honor? Are you not three brothers who are in holy orders and your wives are named Mary after the mother of Jesus?

Now let us view you from various disciplines: According to analytical psychology you have consciousness, personal unconscious, and collective unconscious. Psychoanalysis will tell you that you have ego, id and superego. John don't you have a mind, soul and body, yet you are one person?

After these profound questions, I started researching how the holy Scriptures reveals God as one in three. The very first three verses of the Bible reveal God as one in three: "In the beginning I. God created the heavens and the earth. Now the earth was formless and empty, darkness was over the surface of the deep and the 2. Spirit of God was hovering over the waters, and God 3. Creation was through the Word- God said, let there be light, and there was light. The Creation was through the Word. As the Apostle John puts it: In the beginning was the word, and the Word was with God, and the Word was God. He was with God in the beginning. Through him all things were made, without him nothing was made. The Bible continues to tell us that the Word was light and life. John 1:1-3

The Holy Trinity participated in creation of man. Note that while other creations were through the Word, when it came to the creation of man, God said: Let us make man in our own image, in the image of God he created him, male and female he created them. Thus, man was created by the Holy Trinity as an individual and as a community.

Interestingly, the Kikuyu reported the birth of a baby to the father in both singularity and plurality. For instance, when I was born, the midwife, who was my grandmother, reported to my father: "We have seen men and it is your father-in-law". And there is a Swahili saying: *mtu ni watu*. Meaning a human being is human beings. This means that a human being is created as a unique person, yet he has to give and draw from the community if he is to be healthy and productive

In the following chapters, we will discuss how the trinity is ritualized in our pilgrimage and in our rites of passage [We under go through painful experiences – which result to our spiritual maturity]. We then move from grace to grace.

Chapter One

THE HOLY TRINITY AND VICTORY

My two brothers and I underwent through painful experiences from the Bishops whom analytical psychology terms as "his majesty the baby". The Anglican bishop in Kenya used transfers to punish the priest. Habel had these type of transfers three times. Gideon had similar experience three times. And, as you can see in MINISTRY TO ALL NATIONS and FROM VICTORY TO VICTORY, I was fired three times. The first one I was fired for my accent and africanness and writing the first edition of *CHRIST AND ROOTS;* the second one I was fired for being too ecumenical and the last one for planting an African community Church for the Sudanese and other refugees and by having undesired member of the family living with us in the Vicarage.

Canon Habel's victory came after the retirement. With a fruitful family, he is financially secure and now he attends and minister to all denominations including Roman Catholic where he is occasionally allowed to preach. Gideon enjoys the same financial security and also has partner in mission with two European

Dioceses and is a member of an international religious body known as FIVE TALENTS; which equips the church for economic development. He had a blessing of starting Micro finance program in his diocese and by the time he retired, the diocese had become a billionaire. I always enjoy the way he bides me fare well when I am returning to USA. "As you return to Canaan tell them you have come from Canaan."

When the Holy Trinity gave us the birthday present of All Nations Christian Church International on 7.27.2007, he graciously gave us rest from punitive firings. And, unlimited freedom of service. The Holy Trinity has blessed us with spiritual children in every continent.

Thus, my beloved, if you are going through painful similar experiences, do not lose heart. Remember the loving Father is your shepherd. And, if the loving Father gave victory to three brothers, he will also give you victory. Remember, if you have suffered in Christ, you will also be glorified with him. As you continue fighting a good fight, remember that the Holy Trinity, who has all power and who foreknew what you would go through even before you were born, has provision for you.

Chapter Two

THE HOLY TRINITY AND PROVISION

The Bible tells us that Abraham was visited by three men whom he accorded great welcome and honor. He did three things for them: 1. Bowed down to them 2 gave them water to wash their feet,3 gave them food. The food costed three seahs. They then promised him that he would have a son. When Sara heard that, she laughed. God, who sees everywhere, saw and heard Sarah laughing. And when he asked her why she laughed and asked herself: "After I am worn out and my lord is old, will I have this pleasure?" Then after one year, Sarah had a child. The promise of the Holy Trinity was fulfilled.

Interestingly, it was during the third appearance of Jesus, after the resurrection, that he did the miracle of provision. The disciple had spent the whole night fishing without catching any fish. When Jesus appeared to them and told them to throw the net at the right side, they caught so many fish that they were unable to haul the net in because of the large amount of fish. It was after the catch they recognized that it was the Lord. Better still they found that he has lit fire and prepared fish and the bread for them. It is reported that they caught 153 fish which was the types of fish in the Sea of Galilee. Symbolically Jesus was revealing to them that he will enable them to fish the people of all nations.

Mary and I are awed by the way God provide for us after going through persecution. In the first firing, we were later astonished by God's provision. Since I was denied canonical residence some of my retirement fund was sent to my retirement account in Kenya and other money was kept in a special account. Hence, when I was fired, I had enough money for our expenses in the USA while I looked for a Job.

When I went to Kenya, I took early retirement. I was surprised by the check from Church Commissioners. I never dreamed that someday I would become a millionaire. I was given Kenya shillings which was enough for building six family rental properties. We became more prosperous than we were before we went through fire. Eventually God gave us ministry in Louisiana with the same denomination. The bishop didn't hear our accent and so he put in Church Pension. We however, became more spiritual and ecumenical.

We attended interdenominational early morning prayer service. We started KWANZA celebration for the University. I taught African philosophy and Swahili. We had monthly celebrations of the cultures present in University. By being the only chaplain with three doctorates, the head of the department and graduate's student were coming to me for counseling. We organized overseas missions. Our mission team, which included retired Vice President Dr. Leon Whittaker, ministered in three Kenya dioceses and three Secondary Schools. When we returned, I was surprised to see that they were transformed in such way that they introduced morning prayer breakfast in the University. This of course angered the lay pope who was a master mason. He would latter betray me and I would be fired.

After a short time, I was called to teach at WTA&M University and minister in the university church. The Holy Trinity used us to the maximum. Among other things we taught Biblical studies in the University. We defied the most hated woman in America, Medline O'Hare who through the Supreme Court made it illegal to teach religion the holy trinity and to take the Bible in of public institutions. I told my students, since we were having Biblical studies, they had to bring their Bible. They overjoyed for this freedom. I structured the class in such way that they went through all the Books of the New Testament with the questions: What does this book say about who Jesus is? What does it mean to be a Christian? Many students committed themselves to Christ. We also brought other chaplains together and started United Campus Ministry, of which I was made the President. We also organized walk for Christ in Palo Duro Canyon. We participated in a renewal movement known as Casio.

The Holy Trinity was not surprised when we were fired for reaching out to the Sudanese and having an undesired member of the family living with us. The Holy Trinity, who knew what will happen even before we were born, had a plan for us. When we were evicted from the Vicarage, like in the case of Abraham, he sent three Angles. One angel gave us $2000.00 the second angel gave us $3000.00 and the third angel gave us $5000.00 and we used the money for down payment for our home located at 70 Huntley. Note that the name Huntley has seven letters. So, the message for us is we have to forgive seven times seventy, as our Lord advised. Interestingly, within two years we had seven properties; two were apartments and one was duplex.

The message here is that whatever you lose because of your faithfulness to God, you will be given a hundred-fold. Our greatest joy is that the Holy Trinity graciously gave us a ministry which is international, Interdenominational, and nondenominational and it was officially registered in Texas as an association of churches and ministries on my 65th birthday 7.27.2007. Note the three sevens in the date.

Thus, my beloved, if you are being persecuted for doing what is in keeping with God's will, don't lose heart. Count it all joy. Remember what our precious Savior says: "Blessed are those who are persecuted because of righteousness, for theirs is the kingdom of heaven." Moreover, you need to own this Psalm:

"He said to me, You are my son(daughter) Today I have become your Father.

Ask of me, and I will make the nations your inheritance;

And the end of the earth your possession." Psalm 2:7-8

Amazingly, the Holy Trinity gave us a mission statement:

"Empowered by the Holy Spirit, we preach the Gospel to all nations."

Chapter Three

THE HOLY TRINITY AND TRANSFIGURATION

The story of Jesus' transfiguration has a message about the Holy Trinity. The Gospel tells us that eight days after Peter's great confession of Jesus as Christ, Jesus took Peter, John and James (three disciples) into a mountain to pray. As he was praying his appearance changed and his clothes became as bright as the flash of the lightning." Then Moses and Elijah appeared. Now there were three disciples and three glorified persons. Overwhelmed by the vision Peter said to Jesus: "It is good for us to be here. Let us put three shelters- one for you, one for Moses and one for Elijah. Then the Gospel tells us that Peter didn't know what he was saying. As an extravert, things have to be clear as he talks. The most interesting thing is that Jesus didn't tell the disciples who they were but the disciples were able to recognize that it was Moses and Elijah. Surprising, the description of Jesus is the same as Jesus who appeared to me when I was six years old. Interestingly, so many years later, when I was ministering in Pensacola, Florida, Mary and I visited a white family and the mother of six years told us the story of Jesus who appeared to her six-year-old son. And the vision was very much in keeping in what I saw in the dark room in Ichichi, Kenya.

Astonishingly, I have three persons who have appeared in night visions in the glorified bodies- my mother-in-law Joyce, my auntie Theresa and my Uncle Gideon who took me from our home which was in rural area) to Nakuru where they took care of me for three years. They gave me opportunity to go a trade school, where I learned painting and signwriting. As I have indicated, in this school, the Principal allowed me to teach religious education to all the student from Monday to Friday. They student were calling me bishop. However, the Spirit would not allow me to participate in my auntie's business of selling beer and for that reason I survived with one small meal at night for three years. When my brother Habel who is a soul winner joined me, He won them for Christ and my auntie replaced beer business with keeping animals and my uncle became a landlord. They both became devoted in Christ and joined the Catholic charismatic movement. My uncle was taking Holy Communion every day and gave generously to Church. So, they both rested in the Lord. The vision I had was indicating they are with the Lord. They contributed immensely to my interdenominational, international ethos. In Nakuru we had monthly interchurch service rotating from one church to another ranging from Anglican Church to Salvation Army. We attended the Interdenominational Revival Fellowship. So, my uncle participated in preparing me for the ministry which God has given us.

My mother-in-law, Joyce appeared a night before the ordination of the Rev. Dr. Elizabeth Larson. She was so beautiful wearing white dress with a handbag. Thrilled with her beauty, I told her: "I am not leaving you behind. I am taking you home." She responded. "I cannot go with you this time. I need to study first."

My beloved mother- in- law was my angel during our courtship with Mary and during the bargain for dowry. She reminded Mary, not to be late for her date. During the bargain for dowry, she was my advocate. Before the barging started, she warned the team which was to bargain. "Before you start, I need to tell you that Mary and John will need food after the wedding." My beloved father-in-law responded: " all what I need is a pair of shoes, but this is not a condition." So, we were given blessing to go ahead with wedding even before I bought the shoes. My team was used by God in planning for the wedding party, which cost Ksh270 ($34) which was my monthly salary. We therefore started our life without debt. This was a great miracle of provision, because dowry is highly commercialized. For instant, a young man flew a helicopter to meet with the bargaining team. When they saw the young man with an aircraft, they asked for too much money. The young man became so furious. He jumped into his helicopter and flew away. And, his girlfriend committed suicide. The greedy parents lost their daughter and their son in law. So, my mother-in-law is very dear to me and symbolizes the provision of the Holy Trinity.

The Holy Trinity was using the vision of my mother-in-law to tell the story of Dr. Elizabeth and her husband, Dr. Allen Larson. They have been faithfully supporting our ministry for fifteen years.

Thus, the message in the vision of the appearance of three glorified persons is about the Holy Trinity Who will never forsake those who trust in him. As you read this message, you may be going through hard time. If you are in Christ, he is still saying: "let not your heart be troubled, you believe in God, believed in me also." Solomon has these words for you: "For he will deliver the needy who cry out, the afflicted who have no one to help." Psalm 72:12. Say with David: "He who dwells in the shadow of the Most High, will rest in the shadow of the all mighty. I will say of the Lord: "He is my refuge and my fortress, my God, in whom I trust." Psalm 91:1-2

Chapter Four

THE HOLY TRINITY AND HOLINESS

Holy Trinity is holy. He revealed himself to Isaiah as Holy God. This is what the prophet says: "In the year that king Uzziah died, I saw the Lord seated on the throne, high and exalted and the train of his robe filled the temple. Above him were seraphs, each with six wings (note: 3x2) they covered their faces, with two they covered their feet, and with two they were flying. And they were calling to one another: 'holy, holy, holy is the Lord Almighty. The whole earth is full of his glory." Isaiah 6: 1-3. The sound shook the doorposts and threshold. Note: The seraphs had to cover their faces. Just as six years old Penda covered his face when the Jesus appeared to him at night. Paul was blinded by the light when he was in Damascus road.

What happened to Isaiah? He cried out "Woe to me, I am ruined! For I am a man of unclean lips, and I lived with people with unclean lips, and my eyes have seen the king, the Lord Almighty." Isaiah 6: 5. He repented of his sin and he was cleansed. When the Holy Trinity appeared to me at night in revival fellowship, I confessed my sin. And the Lord graciously forgave me. And as the Word of God puts it: "If we confess our sins, he is faithful and just and will forgive us our sins and cleansed us from all unrighteousness." Not only, that I was cleansed, but I was given power to reject anything which was against the will of God. Then this is power given to all those who are in Christ. Bishop Polycarp for stance, he was given two choices, to deny Christ or else to be burned alive. To this he responded: "For eighty and three years I have served Him; how can I deny my Lord who saved me." He was then burned to death. And of course, so many faithful witnesses have died for their faith. Our joy is that we will be with them forever rejoicing in the Lord.

After repentance and cleansing of sin, the prophet was sent. He was informed that the ministry will not be easy: He was to deal with people who will "be ever hearing but never understand, ever seeing, but never perceiving."

In the case of Moses, when God appeared to him where there was fire which was not burning the bush. God told him to remove his shoes because the place where he was standing was holy. Like Isaiah, when God told him about the mission which he had to undertake. He felt that he was inadequate to face Pharaoh. The Holy Trinity assured him that He will be with him and that he would use the staff which was in his hand. After this assurance Moses felt that he didn't have enough theological education. He even didn't know who God is. The way that God introduced him was even more confusing: God described Himself as I AM WHO I AM. This also means: "I WILL BE WHAT I WILL BE." This reveals the fact that God does not call the qualified; but He qualifies those whom He calls. I remember asking the Principal of our school to get us someone who can teach us religious education and he asked me whether I could teach. When I said I can, he gave me 15 minutes to teach all protestant students. Then, the second semester, he gave me 30 minutes and in the third semester, he gave me 50 minutes. I had not taken any lesson in Religious Education. Twenty-years later I had doctorate in Religious Education. The students whom I taught gave me a title of Bishop. Today I am Archbishop of All Nations Anglican Church and Patriarch of All Nations Christian Church International and Chancellor of ANCCI University. All glory to God.

Thus, when the Holy Trinity calls you, he will prepare and equip you for the ministry he has called to do. When Moses went to Egypt, he was given power, courage and wisdom of dealing with Pharaoh and leading the Israelite through the desert.

When God called Jeremiah, the prophet's response was: "Sovereign Lord, I do not know how to speak, I am only a child." And God responded: "Do not say that 'I am only a child.' You must go to everyone I send you to and say whatever I command you. Do not be afraid of them for I am with you and will rescue you." The Lord also told Jeremiah: "Before I formed you in the womb, I knew you, before you were born, I set you apart to be a prophet to the nations."

Thus, the Holy Trinity assured him that he was a prophet, not only to the Jews but also to the nations. Better still the Lord reached out his hand and touched his mouth and said: "now, I have put my word into your mouth. See, today I have appointed you over the nations and kingdoms to uproot and tear down, to destroy and over through, to build and to plant." Jeremiah 1:4-10

Jeremiah boldly proclaimed the message that God put in his mouth during the reign of Josiah; who was a good king who tried to bring the people of Judah back to God. After Josiah died, Jeremiah continued to proclaim the message of God to Jehoiakim who was as righteous as his father Josiah. Jeremiah prophesied till the eleventh month of Zedekiah to the son of Josiah. Jeremiah faithfully warned the wicked religious and political leaders. He angers them and was persecuted. He was thrown in the pit. An African went to the king and persuaded him to rescue the man of God. He was permitted and rescued Jeremiah. Jeremiah suffered more from priests and false prophets.

Mary and I have suffered more from bishops and lay popes than from secular society. This is now a pure joy, because we learned how to encourage those who are being Jeremiad. The Holy trinity has also given us the right words. Like for instant when we were fired for publishing the first edition of *CHRIST AND ROOTS* and refusing to give Potiphar's wife what she demanded. When we were summoned to the Diocesan headquarter, the bishop with a heavy southern accent said, "You have to go for two things- africanness and accent." The Holy Spirit put the right words in Mary's mouth: She said, "Bishop, let me ask you a question." "Yes Mary." Responded Bishop. "Are you a Christian?" "Yes." Responded the Bishop. "If you are a Christian be listening to good people not to bad people. Be a shepherd to your priests. It can be cold up there." With these words, we departed and never saw the Bishop again. More about this in CHRIST AND ROOTS. The message here, is, like Jeremiah, so many faithful priests have suffered in the hands of bishops who were not Christians. Even though I was the only black in this Diocese, I refuse to conclude that I was fired because I was black. The issue was not the color of my skin but jealousy- For being a Doctor and an author. A few weeks after my firing, another priest who was now the only Doctor in the Diocese was fired. He was white.

Also being a Kenyan American, I had three incidents when I was Jeremiad by the Bishops who were member of my tribe. One of these humiliations happened in my canonical Diocese during the synod. The bishop stared with a roll call (something which has never been seen in the synod.) After the roll call, which included European guest, my name was not there. So, I told the bishop that I didn't hear my name. He responded: "We are going to treat you as a visitor, with no voice and vote." I then left and spent the day at Lake Nakuru Game Park where I had a lovely time with animals and flamingos.

The second humiliation occurred when I had gone on a mission trip with the only white woman Bishop, we have in ANCCI. It happened at the children's home and the church which I founded which was so deer to me that I have put it in my will. So, I went on Saturday and reported to the priest in charge and informed him that we would visit them and share the Word. Reaching the church on Sunday, the priest led us to the office and told us that word has come from the bishop stating that, we cannot preach because we did not follow protocol. We have to sit with the congregation and we will only be allowed to greet people. Thus, the Archbishop and Bishop didn't qualify to be in front seats which are reserved for Lay Readers and priests. So, during the service we were invited to just greet the people. I asked my Bishop to be first. She greeted the congregation without saying a word. When I went in front and said: " let me briefly tell you the history of this church. Many years ago, there was a young man known as Captain John Gatungu. This young man, who was in Christ, is the one who planted this church. Jesus says, "I am the vine, you are the branches, he that abides in me bears much fruit for without me you can do nothing." At this point, I was given a small paper with the message: "time to sit down." The Holy Trinity who knew what would happen had a wonderful plan for us. After this, we attended Messianic Congregation where were well received and allowed to minister. In the evening, we were visited by a Gospel artist from the church which rejected us in the morning. They entertained us with Gospel music.

The third episode took place in the village where I was born. The church is called, St John's, Githiga Memorial Church. When they were deciding the name of the church, the priest who was my father's disciple told the committee that it has to be called Isaac Githiga Memorial Church because Isaac was the one who started Anglican church in the location. It will also be called St. John because Isaac's son John is very committed to Christ. Interestingly, it is only my mother who is buried at church compound. A large number who attended the memorial, were friends and the members of the family who included Bishop Dr. Gideon Githiga, Canon Habel Gitogo, and Rural Dean Paul Wagereka. During this trip, they decided that since John was not able to attend the funeral, he should be the preacher. As we were going in the church, the Diocesan Bishop, who had previously said that he would not be able to attend, popped in. He was told that I was the preacher. He responded: "No, he cannot preach when I am here. I must preach so as to give directives." When he said this, I felt a sharp pain in my umbilical cord. I then quickly asked my glorified mother: "What am I going to do?" She whispered to me: "wichekehie. Which means: "shrink yourself and edge through. "So, with a humble voice I said to the Bishop, "Please allow me to give tribute to my mother." He responded: "Tribute, yes. Preaching no!"

Being first on the program, I took the Bible with me to the podium. The Bishop whispered to my brother Gideon, "Didn't I tell him not to preach? He is now going with the Bible." I then preached for 15 minutes and then invited Mary to come and give the tribute. My dear wife, who is very tactful, invited the key members of the family to come forward and give tribute. After that she gave her tribute. We employed St Martin Luther King philosophy of nonviolent resistance. After this, His Majesty the baby was invited. Little did I know that the directives were to be directed to me. He said: "When you come to Kenya, don't leave all the money in Thika (my brother Gideon's diocese). You must bring some money here." When we were exiting the church, I held Mary's hand as she was still having jetlag and I knew she would trip and fall. His Majesty shouted at me, "Here we do not hold their hands in public!" "So, you let them fall." Mary responded.

Do you see what I see? Have you ever gone through bitter experience which was very similar to other experiences which you had gone through in the same way that you can say: "Here it comes again?" Do you see the counterfeit of the Holy Trinity? You might have been going through It. I still remember, few months after the first firing in the USA, I attend a pastor's fellowship in Mobile Alabama. During the introduction, I said, I have come from a place known as Ichichi, Kenya. I was so surprised too when a pastor, said: "I have been at Ichichi." I have not heard of an American who has visited Ichichi- a place which is like the end of earth- It is next to the forest and mountain. But the greater surprise was to learn that this man of God had just been fired in the same way I was fired.

Do you see the scheme of Satan who is referred to in Genesis as "the craftiest animal? This means he is cunning, sneaky, shrewd, devious and deceitful. He comes at the opportune time when he can hurt you the most. In the case of Jesus, when he was in the desert, he came when he was hungry. Satan asked him to change the stone to be bread. In our case, the enemy came during the most important occasion and at the church which was very dear to us and the memorial of Honorable Joyce who was nicknamed by the neighbor Wagatungu; Gatungu being my given name. The name means the mother and the daughter of Gatungu. As you can also see, St. Nicholas Church was the church which I had planted. See more in *THE HOLY SPIRIT: The Greatest Gift of All.*

But remember that God does not allow the enemy to touch our lives. He was allowed to touch Job's children, and property but not his life. The Great Provider has power to restore all that the enemy has taken. Whatever Stan has destroyed, it was restored seven times. Interestingly as we have shared, all the time when we were fired by the bishops in Episcopal Church, the rationale was that there was no money. And as we have mentioned, after the first firing, we took the early retirement from the Anglican Church of Kenya. We were surprised by the money in Church Commissioner. Our retirement fund was 4 million Kenya shillings. With this money we were able to build six family apartments. And after the third firing and being evicted from the personage, after two years, the Holy Trinity had provided us with seven properties two of which were apartment complex. Better still on 7.27.2007 he gave us a ministry known as All Nations Christian Church International, which is an association of churches and ministry and now we have ministry in every continent.

Thus, as James advises: "Consider it pure joy, my brothers and sisters when you face trials of many kinds, because you know the testing of your faith develop perseverance. Perseverance must finish its work so that you may be mature and complete, not lacking anything." James 1:24. Hence, when we face trials because of our faithfulness in Christ we are lifted to a higher level and we grow in holiness. And, all things, which come to us, leads us to sanctification. As Paul puts it: "And we know that in all things God works for the good for those who love him, who have been called according to his purpose. And those he called, he also justified, and those whom he has called he also glorified."[1] Those who are justified and glorified by the Holy Trinity bears the fruit of the Holy Spirit which is love, joy, peace, patient kindness, gentleness, faithfulness, and self-control.[2] This is all what is required for holiness and fruitful live.

Thus, if you are being persecuted for your faithfulness do remember and own the promise of one who has all authority. This is what he said to the disciples: "All authority in heaven and in the earth has been given to me therefore go and make disciples of all nations baptizing them in the name of the Father and of the Son and of the Holy Spirit and teaching them to obey everything I have commanded you. And surely, I am with you always to the very end of the age." Matthew 28:19 Read more at *CHRIST AND ROOTS and MINISTRY TO ALL NATIONS.*

---

[1] Romans 8:28-31
[2] Galatians 5:22-23

Chapter Five

HOLY TRINITY TRANFORMS THROUGH FIRE

The great story of how the Holy Trinity transforms through fire is in the story of Meshack, Shadrack, Abednego. King Nebuchadnezzar made an image of gold, ninety feet high and nine feet wide and ordered that everyone must worship it and that: "whoever does not fall down and worship will immediately be put into a blazing furnace." Daniel 3:6. When the three young men refused to worship the image, they were reported to the King and then the king called them and ordered them to obey his order or else they will be thrown to the fire. The young men responded: "We do not want to defend ourselves in this matter. If we are put into the blazing furnace, the God we serve is able to save us from it, and he will rescue us from your hand" Then the king ordered them to be thrown into the blazing furnace. The soldiers who threw them in were burned to death. To Nebuchadnezzar's surprise, when he looked what was going on in the fire, he reported the amazing news to his advisers: "Weren't there three men that we tire up and through it the fire? They replied, yes o king." He said: "look, I see four men unbound and unharmed and the fourth looks like a son of gods." Astonished, the King called out: "Shadrack, Meshack and Abednego, servant of the Most High God, come out! Come here." Then the king issued an order that no one should speak anything against God of the three young men.

The three young men were given promotion by the king and the king was transformed. He acknowledges that God of Meshack, Shadrack and Abednego was the Most High God. He also saw the Son of God. He indeed saw Christ who existed before he was born. The profound message for us is, if are in Christ you don't have to fear even when we are going through fire. The Holy Trinity is the fire which burns other fires. This is what the Bible says: "When you pass through the waters, I will be with you; and when you pass through the rivers, they will not sweep over you. When you walk through the fire you will not be burned; the flames will not set you ablaze. For I am the Lord your God, the holy one of Israel, your Savior." Isaiah 43:2-3

Chapter Six

THE HOLY TRINITY HEALS SUPERIORITY AND INFRIORITY COMPLEX

Interestingly, the Holy Trinity, who revealed his power over the fire in saving the three young men, had to deal with Nebuchadnezzar's superiority complex. In the night vision, he saw: "the tree which grew larger and strong and its top touched the sky, it was visible to the end of the earth, its leaves were green, its fruits abundant, and on it were the fruits for all. Under it the beast of the forest found shelter, and the birds of the air lived in its branches, from it every creature was fed." This gigantic tree was cut down. Daniel 4:10-12. Daniel was frightened to give the interpretation of the dream. But the king encourages him to interpret. Daniel, being a true prophet, gave the honest interpretation of the vision. Which revealed that the king will be driven to the forest and eat grass like an animal and will be in this situation seven times (seven years). And so, it happened as Daniel had interpreted the dream. After the painful experience the king was transformed and gave testimony about the greatness of God. He said: "Now I, Nebuchadnezzar, praise and exalt and glorify the King of Heaven, because everything he does is right and all his ways are just. And those who walk in pride he is able to humble." He Thus Worshiped the Almighty God with a song

His dominion is eternal dominion,
His kingdom endures from generation to generation,
All the people of the earth are regarded as nothing.
He does as he pleases
With powers of heaven And the peoples of the earth.
No one can hold back his hand, Or
say to him: "what have you done.
Daniel 4:34-37.

After repenting and worshipping the Most High God; Nebuchadnezzar was restored and his kingdom became even greater.

As I write this chapter, United State is more divided more than ever. This problem grew as the result of superiority complex of Trump and his power base. I was horrified when my sister-in-law in Kenya read a twit from Trump which stated: "White are superior to Arabs and Africans." With this attitude, he refused to secede and motivated white supremist to storm the capital. A person who is suffering from this decease lies to himself that he and his race is superior to other races.

Responding to this attitude, the Kikuyu say: "A proud man thinks that he is more handsome than anybody else." And "He who does not travel, thinks that his mother makes most delicious food." And Bible will say: " Pride come before fall." It is also a person who lives in a small world who judges other people on the basis of accent.

I was startled when I was in Barbados. I had a blessing of giving Holy Communion and baptizing in an Anglican Church. After the service, I stood at the door to greet the brothers and sisters. I was so surprised when lady asked me: "Father Githiga can you speak

English?" I later shared this experience with a British priest who informed me that he was on the same Island and was asked: "Father Michel, can you speak English?" He answered: "We manufactured the language." For Barbadians, on an island 16 miles long and 8miles wide, Barbadian fashion of English is the only English. Hence, we need to forgive those who only hear our accent, because they are basically people who live in their small island and have not interacted with other races.

Being a cultural anthropologist, I have learned that each community has a unique cultural ethos which is beneficial to other communities. The study of Humanities also reveals that each nation has contributed something unique to the global village. From the British Empire we got English. From Arabs we inherited numbers. From the ancient Greek we inherited democracy. From the Roman Empire we got art of government administration and from Africa the meaning and interpretation of symbols and the ecumenical movement.

Thus, the more we draw from international communities, the more we enrich ourselves and expand our ego boundaries.

Mary and I have drawn from many nations. And as I have indicated, we include them in our rites of passage. Remember the prayer of our Lord Jesus Christ: "I pray that all of them may one, Father, just as I am in you. May they also be in us so that the world may believe you have sent me. I have given them the glory that you have given me, that they may one, as we are one." John 17:20-22. The word of God advises us to count others better than ourselves. With this attitude we will be able to give and received.

On the other hand, people who suffer from inferiority complex perceived themselves as poor. They don't think that they have something to give. One of the challenges my wife and I faced when we started ministry to refugees is that they expected to get either from us or white brothers and sisters. One of the most interesting episodes took place after the service. One of them came to me and asked me to get him a TV. I told him that he needed to come to church to pray to God for a job. Then work, get money and then buy the TV. He said: "No! I come to church so that you may pray to God for a TV. He will then give it to you and then you give it to me."

Another man was begging a car. I then found that I have to teach them stewardship. I had to teach them about tithe. To makes it simple I told them, "To tithe simply means: When you get $10, you give $1. When you get $100 you give $10 and when you get $1000 you give $100. At this point I was interrupted by the shout from a woman at the back of the church: "That is too much!"

When we started children's Sunday school, the only people who volunteered were white sisters. To control the children was a great challenge to the teachers. Thus, I had to ask my beloved Sudanese to volunteer to help in controlling their children. No one came forward. I therefore drafted them and prepared the schedule. The day when the schedule was to be implemented none of the persons on schedule came to Church. One of them filled the children in a pickup and dropped them in the parish hall. The white teachers had taken off for summer vacation. Consequently, a twelve years old girl put his six years old brother on a wheel chair to train him to fly. The wheel chair was broken. When the hosting church found the broken wheel chair, the church council was convinced and resolved that we will never use the church again, effective from the day that the resolution was made. Hence, I was called by the Rector on Thursday and informed that we would not use the church on Sunday. It was a real headache to figure out how to communicate to 150 members that we could not use the church on Sunday. Moreover, I had a full-time job with the University Church which was giving us salary. We were not getting anything from the refugee's congregation. I was also teaching Biblical studies at the University for free and I had papers to grade. I must admit that on Saturday of that week, I had a headache and was somewhat mixed up. Attending the occasion where Mary was being honored for 12 years of ministry to sick and dying through Hospice, I found myself in the wrong restroom where I discovered that my next-door neighbor was a woman. After this I visited Pastor Daryl of Fellowship Freedom Church who prayed for me and was instantly healed. He then prayed that the very first telephone I will call, I get information about where my refugees' church will worship on Sunday. When I went home, I called a priest who was friend of mine and within 30minutes he called me and told he has found a church for us. We have been worshipping in this church for 17 years.

This story is about how God deals with our superiority complex and inferiority complex. As someone who has five theological degrees, God has to let me go through the wilderness which has to make me humble. The priest who kicked us out of the church also went through this bitter experience. After he kicked us out, most of his members left the church and after one year he was fired for caring more about the building than the parishioner. And after one year he was dead.

The six-year-old who was being trained by his sister to be a pilot, he is now with United States Air Force. And his sister is doing community development ministry in Sudan and Father Dr. Simon Aluak is Director of Revenue services in Southern Sudan.

Eventually we started ANCCI University which gave theological education to the refugee pastors. And today, they have planted 135 churches in America, Canada, and Sudan.

I should admit that there was part of me that appeared primitive to them. On one occasion we were having party in the home of one of the members. The host tried to call the meeting to order but everybody was busy talking to each other. I then whistled as I used to do when I was a herd boy so as to get the attention of the castles.

To my great surprise everybody was quite. I then thought I had hit the right button. The women came quietly from the kitchen and ask: "who made that noise?" Abuna (Father in Arabic). She then said: "In my country that noise is made by homeless." So as a missionary do realize that there is a part of you which is inferior to the people of the other culture. And thus, it has to be each one teaches one.

Our great joy is that the church which was kick out known as African Community Church which is pastored by our Spiritual son, Mabur Atak, has a church building with a parsonage. And it is very orderly. They start with children Sunday school and all the teachers are Sudanese. On Christmas of 2020, I had a blessing of launching our books. Not only that, everything was orderly. They bought so many books. And being Mary's birthday, she was given so much money which she has never received as a birthday gift. The lesson for us is we have to be patient. Apostle James advise us : "Be patient brothers until the Lord's coming. See how the farmer waits for the land to yield its valuable crops and how patient he is for the autumn rains. You too be patient and stand farm because the Lord's coming is near." James 4:7-8.

As we shall see later, the way to heal from with Superiority complex or inferiority complex is to love God will all your mind, with all your strength and your neighbor as ourselves. After being in the wilderness and eating grass like an animal Nebuchadnezzar recognized the Creator of all things as the Most High God.

Chapter Seven

HOLY TRINITY AND SUPERNATURAL PROTECTION

Daniel was getting visions and ability of interpreting dreams through the power of God whom he prayed three times daily. Note that he was dramatizing the Holy Trinity by worshipping **three times.** His effectiveness and progress made the diviners and wise men of Babylon jealousy of him. Jealousy can be defined as negative and destruction emotion toward a successful person. So those who wanted to destroy him accused him to the king. The kings, who has to do something against his will, permitted Daniel to be thrown into the den of lions. The Bible tells us: He returned to his palace and spent the night; 1. Without eating, 2. Without any entertainment being brought to him, and 3. He could not sleep. Note: The three things which happened to the king. The very first thing he did was at: "the first light at down the king hurried to the lions' den. When he came near the den, he called to Daniel with anguished voice, 'Daniel, servant of the living God, has God, whom you serve continually, been able to rescue you from the lions?'" Daniel answered, "O king, live forever. My God sent his angel and he shut the mouth of the lions." The king, overjoyed gave order that Daniel be lifted from the lions' den. He ordered his accusers to be thrown into the den. The Bible tells us that the "lions overpowered them and crushed all their born."

As you read this chapter, you may be going through persecution from Judas, or you may know a faithful minister of the Gospel who is going through betrayal. The author knows of a Baptist minister in the city where he was ministering. This man of God was betrayed by **three Judases** (trinity counterfeit) . They finally had him fired. Soon after the firing the minister was called by a parish which gave him triple of the stipend which he was getting. God, who is faithful and powerful Judge took action. One of the Judases was fired from his job. The second Judas became blind. The third Judas had heart attack and died.

At the same time a minister know as Padre Penda and his wife were being persecuted by a Judas who was a master mason, who's ideal was in contrast to those of Penda. For the Masons **three things** are most important- 1.money, 2power 3 sex-which includes sexual immorality. The Judas accused Penda of being too ecumenical. The battle was so fierce that Penda developed high blood pressure. On a particularly day, Penda was driving home from a Diocesan convention. Realizing that he is going to face the same Judas, he talked to God. "God, how long will let this man sabotage your ministry? It is not my ministry. It is your ministry." Arriving home, the first call came from the wife of this man reporting that her husband is dead. The man was not sick. But God took immediate action. The man had instructed his family that when he died, he would not like to be buried by Padre and thus the family invited a white priest, who ministered in the parish before Penda. This priest, whom Judas had had him fired, gave a short homily which was directed to the Judas: "You have wrestled with power in the church and the University. You are now going to face Him who has all power."

If you are being persecuted by Judas do not lose heart. All, who is all powerful, knows what you are going through. He will use the experience to glorify Himself and make you bear much fruits. This is what he did with Daniel. Not only that he rescued Daniel, but he won the King and his Kingdom to Himself. This is what King Darius says: To all the peoples, nations, and men of every language:

May you prosper greatly…

I issue a decree that in every part of my kingdom people must fear and worship the God of Daniel.

For the living God and he endures forever;
His kingdom will not be destroyed,
His dominion will never end;
He rescuers and saves,
He performs signs and wonders;
In all heaven and earth
He has rescued Daniel from the power of lions.

Consequently, Daniel prospered during the reign of Darius and Cyrus the Persian.[3]

The message for us is that if we fight a good fight and be faithful to the end, God will bless us and make us fruitful. Thus, let us sing with the Psalmist:

Give thanks to the Lord, call on his name;
Make known to the nations what he has done.
Sing to him, sing praises to him.
Tell of all his faithful acts. Psalm 105:1-2

---

[3] Daniel 6:25-28

Chapter Eight

HOLY TRINITY AND VICTORY OVER PERSECUTION

The Holy Trinity, being the creator of all that is and who has power to destroy everything, and gives the Saint victory over fear and pain during the persecution. The story of Shadrack, Meshack and Abednego shows how God gave them victory over fear and how God protected them from fire. The Holy Trinity is the fire which burns other fires. We also saw how He shut the mouth of the lions and could not harm Daniel.

During the Kenya war of independent, Mau Mau, who were freedom fighters, associated Jesus with white men and for that reason, they administered oath which required Christians to deny Christ. Those who were in Christ preferred to die rather than denying Christ. One of these witnesses was Andrew Kaguru, who was a disciple of my father. They broke the doors of his house at night and demanded that he deny Christ. Andrew, full of the Holy Spirit, told them: "I cannot deny Christ. What you want to do, do it quickly. They then killed him and I believe he immediately went to heaven. The other two who survived to tell their story were Samuel and Sara Muhoro. The killers broke their door at night and started to cut Samuel with butcher's knife. While they were doing that, Sarah full of the Holy Spirit, smiled at the killers. When they saw her smiling, they said: "Why are you smiling at us? Don't you know that we are killers?" She responded: " I know, but Jesus loves you". They then stopped killing Samuel and went to the bedrooms and took all the blankets. Sarah, full of peace said to them: "Folks, don't forget that we have children." They then threw some of the blankets to her and said: "be praying for us." Samuel who survived to tell the story said that when he was being cut, I was not feeling pain.

Another couple was killed for their faith. The killers came at night. The wife was six months pregnant. When the persecutors broke in and asked them to deny Christ or else, they will die. The pregnant Christian woman was first to respond: "This baby will be born in heaven." They were both killed. I do believe we will see the baby in heaven. Not as a baby, but as a glorified adult human being.

I have a discipline of daily reflection of the Saints. One of the most impressive saints is St Agnes who was a very beautiful young woman. The governor who was attracted to her wanted to marry her by force. When she refused, she was told that she has to either marry the governor or be beheaded. Her response was: "I will not marry him. And those who will kill me will be only stain their sword. "It is said that she was more joyous on the day of her death, than she could have been during her wedding day.

Another Saint who has impacted on me is Bishop Huntington who was killed in Mombasa by the king of Uganda. When the soldiers from Uganda were killing him, before he died, he said to them, "Go and tell the king that my blood has prepared the road for salvation to Uganda." Huntington planted the East African Revival Movement, which brought me to Christ 64 years ago. And it was in Easter African fellowship we were nurtured in Christ. And

I believed it is because the seed which Huntington planted that you are able to read this book. I believe that I am a theologian, because of what Christ has done and is still doing for me.

The message in this chapter is that the Holy Trinity will be with us during persecution. He imbues us with courage and gives us the right words. This is why Jesus advises us not to think before what we will say, for we will be given the right words and courage. I am surprised by the song which the Holy Trinity put in my mouth when I was undergoing persecution in Nakuru, Kenya for three years. I survived by having one small meal in the evening because. I was so thin and looked like walking skeleton. Ironically, these were the most joyous days of my life. And with the power of the Holy Spirit, I preached the gospel to all races. The song that God gave me was:

The greatest treasure;
The greatest peace;
The greatest joy
Is the Lord Jesus

You who are carrying heavy load;
With so many excuses
Come to Jesus;
And he will give you rest.

Are you listening to his voice?
He is calling you now;
To purify your heart;
And give you victory over sin.

When I was given that song, I was feeling plugged in the universal energy, which was both transcendent and immanent. With this power I reached out to all tribes, Indian and Europeans. I was not even scared to visit families at night. One interesting episode took place in a home of someone who was taking drugs.

He remarked: "You are very lucky. You came when I had not taken my drug. Otherwise, you couldn't come out arrive."

Being a very skinny teenager, Satan ridiculed me: "look how skinny you are." To respond to this, I composed a song for the body.

> The body we have is not perfect.
> It is made of dust.
> But it should not keep us from heaven
> Thou live and die we must.
>
> From dust it was made by our father.
> Dust it shall it shall become.
> This body we have is not perfect.
> For us or for anyone.
>
> Now those who will trust in the Father.
> He will raise to be.
> In wonderful perfect new bodies
> With him eternally.

These songs motivated me to focus on the power of the Holy Trinity. And exerted the spiritual energy in preaching the Gospel. The other song which motivated me was:

> There is nothing too hard for thee dear Lord.
> Nothing. Nothing.
> There is nothing too hard for thee.

Thus, when we are facing persecution, let us remember the words of our Lord: "Blessed are you when people insult you, persecute you and falsely say all kinds of evil against you because of me. Rejoice and be glad, because great is your reward in heaven, for in the same way, they persecuted the prophets who were before you." Matthew 5:11-12

Chapter Nine

THE HOLY TRINITY AND MISSION TO THE GENTILE

Jonah was commanded by the Holy Trinity to go to Nineveh, but instead he rebelled and ran way and headed to Tarshish, which was opposite direction. Then God sent a great storm. The ship crew and everybody prayed to God while Jonah was asleep. When the crew found that everybody was praying while Jonah was sleeping, they suspected that he was the cause of the problem. Thus, the captain went to Jonah and asked "How can you sleep? Get up and call on your God! May be he will take notice of us, and we will not perish." Then the sailor cast the lot to find out who was the cause of the calamity. It fell on Jonah. At this point the gentiles were the heroes and godlier than Jonah, the Jew. The crew asked Jonah: "Tell us who is responsible for making all this trouble for us. What do you do? Where do you come from? Then Jonah responded: "I am a Hebrew and I worship the Lord, the God of heaven, who mad the sea and land." The crew learned that he was running away from God. Then they asked Jonah what they should do and then he told them to throw him to sea. He was then swallowed by the fish and was in the belly of the fish for **THREE**

DAYS. Here God is revealing himself as the Holy Trinity and the God of all nations. He revealed to the gentile that Jonah was the problem. Nevertheless, God did not forsake Jonah, He protected him and Jonah was vomited onto the dry land in Nineveh and gave him energy for preaching for **THREE DAYS**. His mission was very successful. The whole city, including the King committed themselves to God.

After a great and successful mission, Jonah was depressed and became suicidal. He was even angry with God. He cried out: "Is this not what I said while I was still at home? That is why I was so quick to flee to Tarshish. I know that you are gracious and merciful God, slow to anger and abounding in love, a God who relent from sending calamity. Now, oh Lord, take away my life, for it is better for me die than to live." Jonah 4:1-3.

Viewing Jonah problem from clinical theology perspective, the major problem of this prophet was lack of spiritual partner. Jesus, being as powerful as he was, he had spiritual partners. He had Martha, Mary and Lazarus. He had Peter, John and Andrew. Paul had spiritual partners- Beloved physician Luke, Timothy, Titus and Mark. At one time the door for mission was open, because he could not enter because his spiritual partner, Titus was not there. In my case, I have benefitted immensely from the spiritual partners. We normally meet weekly, read the word of God and pray together.

The other problem was that Jonah lacked a spiritual Director. On one occasion when I was in the University of the South, I was counseling a woman who, at one time, gave me a card after the session. I put the card in the pocket of my jacked without reading it. Few days later, I got a call informing me that my client has committed suicide. I then remembered that she had given me a card. Opening the card, I found interesting message:

"Father Githiga, you are great and I am grateful." I had to ask myself: "If I am great and she is grateful, why did she commit suicide?" When I was approaching depression, I visited my spiritual director who gives light in my confusion. He informed me that I was a massager; not a Messiah. The session helped me to gain my sanity. I also did research on the great men who committed suicide. This included Samson, who killed himself with one thousand philistines. The message here is that we need spiritual partners and spiritual Directors.

We also need to obey God, regardless the consequence of our mission. As I have mentioned I started evangelism when I was a teenager. I still remember an episode, which took place when I was seventeen. I was visiting my sister Mary in Naivasha. After a lighting the bus, I saw police village with fifty-two homes. I was commanded by the Holy Trinity to enter each and every house and tell the families whatever the Lord will put in my mouth. As I was entering the fourth house, I was intoxicated with joy and the power of the Holy Spirit. When I was getting out of the last house, the police officer who was furious asked me: "Who are you and who gave you permission to enter the police homes? I responded: "I am the son of the King of Kings and I was commanded by the King to do so." The office shouted to me: "Get away from hear." At this rebuke, my cup started overflowing with oil and I was full of the joy and the peace of God which surpasses all understanding.

Chapter Ten

THE HOLY TRINITY AND BLESSING

The story of Balaam and the donkey reminds me of an episode which took place when I was seven years. I was herding a donkey. We reached in the place where it was between the fences. I was behind the donkey which gave me a kick. I flew in the air, fell and saw the stars and then laid unconscious for a long time. When I woke up, I didn't see the donkey and I never saw it again. In the case of Balaam, he had been summoned by the king of Moab to go and curse the Israelites. The Bible tells us that " God was very angry when he went and the angel of the Lord stood on the road to oppose him when the donkey saw the angel of the Lord standing in the road with a drawn sword in his hand, she turns off the road into a field. But Balaam beat her to get her back on the road." When Balaam beat her the **THIRD TIME,** the donkey spoke to the prophet and said: What have I done to you to beat me these three times? Note: Three times. Then Balaam told the donkey, "You have made a fool of me! If I have a sword in my hand, I would kill you right now." The donkey responded, "Am I not your own donkey, which you have already ridden, to this day? Have I been in the habit of doing this to you? "No," he said. "Then the Lord opened the eyes of Balaam and he saw the Angel standing in the road with a sword." This three experiences and conversation with a donkey open the eyes of Balaam and he was transformed from cursing to blessing. In his first oracle he said: "How can I curse those whom God has not cursed?" Rather than cursing them he preferred to die with them: "Let me die the death of the righteous and my end be like theirs." Barak was not pleased and he gave more gifts. But Balaam obeyed God who is unchangeable. He said: "I have received a command from him to bless. He has blessed and I cannot change it." In the third oracle he blessed them, "May those who bless you be blessed and those who curse you be cursed." In the fourth and the last oracle, Balaam predicted that Israel will have final victory. (See Numbers 23-24).

This story has profound meaning for us all and particularly to those who are called to preach the Gospel. The message is that the Holy Trinity can use various means to reveal his will for us. The story of the donkey, which kicked the herd boy, shows us how a pastor can suffer from the very people that he is shepherding. As the Swahili proverb puts it: "The donkey's gratitude is a kick. (Asante ya punda ni teke). During many years of shepherding Mary and I have been given kick by the very sheep that we shepherded. And from the bishops who are supposed to shepherd the shepherds. As we have mentioned, the first firing we were told that I have to go because of "Africanness and accent." We had developed the parish spiritually, in membership, stewardship and involvement in the community. Our ministry was accompanied by signs and wonders. More about this in *CHRIST AND ROOTS* and *MINISTRY TO ALL NATIONS* and *FROM VICTORY TO VICTORY.* As analytical psychologist, I learned that the bishop who fired the priests for their achievement were those analytical psychology terms: His Majesty the baby. He has power without adequate education. They are also those who were described by Jesus as foolish virgins who has lamp without oil. They have no Holy Spirit. They like also siding with Judas in the congregation as did the priests who had Jesus arrested.

If you are being persecuted either by Judas or his majesty the baby, do realize that you are not alone. Like Balaam, do not compromise the prophecy. Know that the one who is in you is greater than those who are in the world. If his majesty the baby hates you because of your fruitful ministry there is a Kikuyu proverb which is very encouraging: "Haria ikagio tiho iguage." The enemy does not fall where it is thrown. The Holy Trinity who sees things before they happen and is all powerful will send his angels to protect and to provide for you. As I was working on this chapter, Dr Gideon Githiga shared our painful experiences and the appearance of the Angels. When Gideon was a warded scholarship for PhD program in United Kingdom, he was thrown away by his bishop. The Holy Trinity provided him with three angels. One of the Angels was Archbishop David Gitare who gave him the required ecclesiastical endorsement. The two angels provident housing stipend for the family. And as you will see, in my third firing God provided us with three angels who provided us with the fund for down payment of our home. And within three years we had seven properties. So, if you are undergoing through challenges, the Bible says: "And we know that in all things God works for the good of those who love him, who have been called according to his purpose… in all these we are more than conquerors through him who loved us." Roman 8:28, Further more Paul advises: "Do not be anxious about anything, but in everything by prayer and petition, with thanksgiving, present your request to God. And the peace of God which transcends all understanding will guard your mind and hearts in Christ Jesus." Philippians 4: 6-7

Chapter Eleven

THE HOLY TRINITY AND BAPTISM OF JESUS

Interestingly, the word Trinity is not found anywhere in the Bible.

Yet, the God who has revealed himself in Threeness is found in many places in the Old and the New Testament. During the baptism of Jesus, the Bible says: " When all people were being baptized, Jesus was baptized too. As he was praying, the heaven was open. And the Holy Spirit descended on him in bodily form like a dove. And a voice came from heaven: "You are my Son, whom I love, with whom I am well pleased."[4]

Here we see the presence of God the Father, God the Son and God the Holy Spirit. God the Father says three things about the Son, 1.My Son. 2 Whom I love. 3.And with whom I am well pleased. And then he was led by the Spirit to the desert.

Note that in the desert there were three: Satan, wild animals and angels. During our pilgrimage we undergo through many desert experiences. We find ourselves in a situation when we are neither in

[4] Matthew 3:13-17

Egypt nor the Promised Land. We find people who are very much like wild beast. Satan uses them to test us. And being the craftiest of all the beasts, he comes at the opportune time. He waited for Jesus to be hungry. Then he came up with three temptations: 1. If you are the Son of God, tell this stone to become bread. Use your divine power for self-satisfaction. Concentrate only on prosperity Gospel and never talk about the cross. Tell people what they would like to hear so that you may get what is in their pocket. To this Jesus responded, "It is written man does not live by bread alone but by every word that comes from the mouth of God."[5] Hence, to conquer the devil in this temptation we have to read the word of God and pray every day. One of the greatest gifts that God has given me is a wife who reads the word of God every day. We do this before breakfast. We start with a prayer: "Open my eyes that I may behold wonderful things in your word." Psalm 119:18.2.

The second temptation: "The devil led him up to a high place and showed him in an instant all the kingdom of the world. And he said to him: 'I will give you all the authority and splendor, for it has been given to me and I can give it to anyone I want."[6] Satan, being the father of lies is now lying to Jesus that all things belong to him. Yet in fact "All things were made through the Word, and without him, nothing was made."[7] The problem of miss use of power has caused afflictions of the faithful prophets. Jeremiah was thrown into dish for his prophecy. Yet God rescued him, and in the end his prophecy was fulfilled and the nobles were taken to exile in Babylon, and Jeremiah was given freedom to either go to Babylon or remain in Jerusalem. He chose to remain in Jerusalem. As you read this message, you may be going through what all true prophets went through. As you can see in *MINISTRY TO ALL NATIONS,* when we were being fired for our accent and Africanness, the Holy Spirit gave Mary a word of wisdom to respond to the Bishop. After the judgment she asked him: "Bishop, let me ask you a question. Are

---

[5] Matthew 4:1-11; Deuteronomy 8:3; Luke4:4
[6] Luke 4:1-13;
[7] John 1:1-4

you a Christian?" "Yes Mary." Responded the Bishop. Then Mary, as a daughter of the King, had last word: "If you are a Christian, be listening to good people and not bad people." And of course, after the firing, one of the spiritual Christians who was a professor in the University visited with Bishop and asked him why he has fired their priest. The bishop responded: "It is not me. It is the church council." A few days later, a woman who had accused the priest, called and asked for forgiveness for lying to the bishop about him.

Hence, if you suffer for being a true prophet, do not loose heart or judge the whole church because of Judas. If you are of different race from the bishop don't judge the whole race because of one person. Note that the church is the only institution which comprises of members and nonmember, goats and sheep, tares and good seed. If you are the one who is tempted to misuse your power. Shout to Satan: "It is written, worship the Lord your God and worship him only." Stop worshipping the self. If you opt to remain His Majesty the baby, you will pay a heavy price. As you will see, the sons of Isaac Githiga who are in holy orders, underwent through three punitive transfers and of course, the other had three punitive firing. In all cases, the bishop sided with Judases. Like Judas who complained that the expensive perfume which was poured on Jesus, should have been sold and the money be given to the poor. And John informs us that Judas said this not because he cared about the poor but because he was a thief who stole the money which was given for the ministry.[8] He also betrayed Jesus for money. He however, ended committing suicide.

Those who gave Canon Habel punitive transfers incurred God's judgment. They all died lonely. In my case, as I have noted, one of Judases died before, I was fired. He didn't get sick, but I remember coming back from Diocesan convention. As I was driving home, I remembered that I was going to face the lay pope. I asked All Powerful Judge: "How long, will you let this man sabotage your

---

[8] John 12: 1-8

ministry? It is not my ministry. It is your ministry." The very first call I got when I arrived home was from Judas's wife who reported to me that the man was dead. Before he died, he had instructed his wife that if he died, Father Githiga should not conduct his funeral. We then had to invite a former white priest, whom the lay pope had had fired. The funeral homily from the priest was precise and directed to the man in the coffin: "You have wrestled with powers. Powers in the church. Powers in the university. You are now going to face, He who has all powers." Hence, if you are a priest killer, you will indeed face the one who has all powers.

If you are the one who is facing Judas and wild animals. Do not lose heart. Know that you have a High Priest who went through the same kind of things and who is at the right hand of God. Be assured that in the end, you will be a winner. As I am writing this chapter, I visited with Canon Habel, who shared with me an experience in the retired prison officers' home in which Judas and Senior Chaplain lived. They had transferred Habel three months before his retirement. The former Senior Chaplain who was so sick told Canon; I know you cannot remember me." Habel was not recognizing the man, for he was so sick. But my brother, who always attend the meeting with his cleric color and had volunteered to be a preacher. After the Sermon, the retired Senior Officer asked a person who was Judas, to take off his cup and collect the offering for the preacher.

Does this remind you Psalm 23: 5? "You prepare the table for me in the presence of my enemies. You anoint my head with oil, my cup overflows. Surely goodness and mercy will follow me all the days of my life. And I will dwell in the house of the Lord forever." Hence, be assured that whatever was taken away from you by Judas and the priest killer, the Lord will restore to you a hundredfold. You will achieve this if you keep on reading your Bible and praying every day in Holy Spirit.

Chapter Twelve

HOLY TRINITY AND DOUBT

The eleven disciples went to Galilee, to the mount where Jesus had told them to go; "And when they saw him, they worshiped him: but some doubted." Matthew 28:16-17

Jesus had to give the Great Commission, within the context of doubting disciples. Then he had to further tell them what He is and what they must be and do. He has all authority. "All authority in heaven and on earth has been given to me. Therefore, go and make the disciples of all nations baptizing them in the name of the Father, the Son and the Holy Spirit. And teaching them to observe everything I have commanded you. And surely, I am with you always, to the very end of the age. Mt 28:18-20.

Did you know that the Holy Trinity calls us to do what is humanly speaking impossible and that most great men of God started their mission with doubt? When Moses was call to liberate the Israelites, his first reaction was: "Who am I, I even don't know how to speak." Jeremiah reaction was: "I do not know how to speak; I am only a child." Isaiah's reaction was: "I am a man of unclean lips and I live among the people with unclean lips and my eye has seen the King, the Lord Almighty." Isaiah 6:5. God revealed himself to Isaiah as a Holy Trinity. He heard the seraphs singing: *"Holy, holy, holy is the Lord Almighty, the whole earth is full of his glory."*

God still use three to call us and commission us for a particularly ministry and also to get us out of a particular box. As I have mentioned, when God was preparing us for ministry with and to all nations, we underwent three nasty experiences. During the third firing I had so many questions: Why am I a priest, the profession, which at this time is the most unholy institution? We're not the high priests who persecuted Jesus and the early Christian. "Why am I being fired after being an answer to the denominal prayer which had prayed worldwide, using the Anglican Prayer cycle, for the Church in Sudan? Am I not a member of the communion of saints who are defined as: "a great multitude which no one can count from every nation, tribe, and language?" (Revelation 7:9.) Is it theological correct to save the money from the only black priest in the Diocese? However, I had no one to answer my questions and as painful as the experience was, it led me to transformation both in the Diocese and in us. The parishes which were spiritual and biblically based departed from the Diocese and joined African Mission in America under the oversite of Archbishop Alex Bilindabagambo of Rwanda, who was my student at St. Paul University. Other orthodox churches including St. Cyprian's International Church joined Thika Diocese under the oversite of Bishop Gideon, my brother. And eventually God commanded us to start All Nations Christian Church International which was registered in Texas as association of churches and ministries on 7.27.2007 which was my 65th birthday. Later on, we started ANCCI University which educated pastors from different church families. These include refugees' pastors who have planted one hundred and thirty-five churches. All **glory to God.**

Chapter Thirteen

THE HOLY TRINITY IS IRSISTABLE LIGHT

Jesus claimed, "I am the light of the world. Whoever follows me will never walk in darkness, but will have the light of life."[9] One of the names of the Kikuyu God is *Mwenenyaga.* The word refers to the brightness of the snow at the peak of Mount Kenya which is the highest mountain in Kenya. At the peak of the mountain there is a snow-the only snow which is known by the Kenyans. So *Mwenenyaga* is the being with unique brightness.(more about this in *CHRIST AND ROOTS).* Thus, the Holy Trinity is the being with the Irresistible light. I still remember as thou it happened last night, the Being of Light who appeared to me when I was six-years-old. I was sleeping in a very dark room, when he appeared to me. I did three things: 1. I closed my eyes so that I may not see the light. The light remained visible. 2. I then covered my closed eyes with a blanket. But I continued seeing the Being of Light. 3. I then put the palms of my hands on the top of the blanket, but a continued seeing the Being of Light. The next day I gave my first sermon to my friend as we were herding. I asked my friend to close his eyes

---
[9] John 8:12

and then look direct to the sun. He did. I asked him whether he saw anything. He said no.

I then told him of the being who appeared to me last night and how I covered my eyes and continued seeing him.

Paul encounter with the Being of Light was more dramatic than mine. He had gotten authorization letter to go to arrested Christian. On Damascus Road, the being of light appeared to him with a question: "Saul, Saul why do you persecute me." "Who are you, Lord?" He asked. "I am Jesus whom you are persecuting... now get up and you will be told what you must do."[10] Paul had several threes. 1. He is no longer in control. 2. He must do what is told. 3.He got up from the ground. Three things happened to him. 1 He was blind and for three days he could not see. 2. He ate nothing. 3 He drank nothing. He had total obedience to the Holy Trinity. Saul was given a new name- Paul. He was changed from being a persecutor of the people of the Way, to someone who courageously preach the Gospel with total obedience to the Holy Trinity. From some who looked down upon the gentile, to someone who was will to suffer for them.

When we commit ourselves fully to the Holy Trinity through Christ, we become children of the light. And as the Bible says: "In him was life, and that life was the light of men. The light shines in the darkness, but the darkness has not overcome it."[11] Those who have received the light are given right to became children of God. Children of light don't have to fear the darkness. They have overcome the world. If you are a child of light, you need to scare the darkness with these words:

"The Lord is my light and my salvationWhom shall, I fear?
The Lord is the stronghold of my life-
Of whom shall I be afraid?" Psalm 27:1

---
[10] Acts 9:1-9
[11] John 1:1-5

Chapter Fourteen

HOLY TRINITY AND GREATCOMMISSION

In the great commission, Jesus says to the disciples: "All authority in heaven and on earth has been given to me, therefore go and make disciples of all nations, baptizing them in the name of the Father and of the Son and of the Holy Spirit and teaching them to obey everything that I have commanded you. And surely, I am with you always, to the very end of the age." Matthew 28:18-20. These words of our Lord are just as important as the last words of parents. In these words, Jesus reveals God as the Holy Trinity who will be with us always. This is why we baptize in the name of the Father, and of the Son and of the Holy Spirit. This implies that to be a Christian is to believe in the Holy Trinity. When the Holy Trinity is in us, we are given power and authority for holy living and for preaching the Gospel. Before he ascended to heaven he promised: "And you shall receive power, when the Holy Spirit comes on you, and you will be my witnesses in Jerusalem, and in all Judea and Samaria, and the end of the earth." Acts 1:8 The subtitle of our book *THE HOLY SPIRIT* is: *The Greatest Promise, And the Greatest Gift of All*. It is the greatest promise because it was fulfilled few days after Jesus ascended to heaven.

There were visible signs: "When the day of Pentecost has come, they were all together in one place. 1. Suddenly a sound like the blowing of the violent wind came from heaven and filled the whole house where they were sitting. 2. They saw what seemed like the tongue of fire that was separated and came to sit on each one of them. 3 All of them were filled by the Holy Spirit and began to speak in other tongues as the Spirit enabled them." Acts 2:1-4 You can see the three phenomena. But more importantly, the transformation which took place included speaking in other languages and the miracle of the ear.

When I was in Grambling LA, I attend a black church. After the sermon, the preacher who was Spirit filled led the people to pray. One woman was filled with the Holy Spirit and prayed in other tongues. Being the only African, I understood the language which she spoke and I still remember what she said: Nyasai. Nyasai. Nyasai. Which means: "Oh God! Oh God! Oh God!" She was speaking Luo, one of the languages spoken in Kenya. It should however be pointed out that speaking in tongue and interpretation are the gifts on the Holy Spirit. Therefore, we should not expect every Spirit filled Christian to either speak or interpolate in tongue. When our cups are being filled, we have different manifestation. Mary speaks in tongues. While in my case I shade tears. My Brother Habel fills a great urge of winning souls for Christ. He has won so many members of our family. When he was chaplain in prison, he won so many inmates including condemned prisoners. One of the inmates told my brother, "Teacher. My situation is even better than yours because I know exactly the day and the time when I will go to heaven. Habel has to be with the prisons when they are being hanged so as conduct their funeral. This would be too hard for me. I could possibly collapse with the person. But Habel had charisma of doing that. The most important thing is fulfilling the great commission: Preaching the Gospel to all nations and winning them for Christ and baptizing them in the name of Father, and of the Son and of the Holy Spirit.

Chapter Fifteen

THE TRINITY AND GOOD SAMARITAN

It is awesome to discover trio in the parable of the Good Samaritan which was an answer to the question of a lawyer who was testing Jesus by asking what he must do to inherit eternal life. Jesus answered by asking a question: "What is it written in the law?" The expert of the law was very precise: " 1.Love the Lord your God, 2 with all your soul and with all your strength and 3 And love your neighbor as yourself. Jesus answered: "you have answered correctly. Do this and you will live." Then Jesus gave him the most famous parable about the Good Samaritan.[12] Note that in the story there are three characters. The priest and the Levites who by passed the suffering man. Then the Samaritan who had compassion and took care of the robbed and wooded person. The priests and the Levites were the most respected persons in the community. But the Samaritans were looked down upon by the Jews. Jews even avoided passing through Samaria. They would not associate with them or even eat with them. And this was because they were mixt race. They intermarried with the Gentiles and so in the eye of the Jews, the Samaritans were unclean.

---
[12] Luke 10:25-37

But Jesus, not only reached out to a Samaritan woman, but he won her for the kingdom and made her an apostle (the word means one who is sent) to the other Samaritan. They came to Jesus and their testimony was: "woman, we no longer believe because of what you have said, now we have heard for ourselves. And we know that this man is really the savior of the world." And Jesus and his disciple stayed with the Samaritan for two more days. John 4:1-43.

Where the Holy Spirit fills every fiber of our being, there is a give and take between the people of different races. Mary and I, being the only African American in the neighborhood, have experience grace after grace. We had a police officer who mowed our yard. After almost year of lock in because of covin19, this police office paid us a visit. He made sure he hugged us twice. We read Psalm 23 together. When I was working on this chapter, his wife visited with us and gave us doughnuts and we had lovely visit. Don't forget that it was an African who helped Jesus to carry the cross[13]. If you are in the place where your race is looked down upon, see yourself in the light of the word of God. Say to yourself. "I am made in the image of God." "I am wonderfully and fearfully mad." "God loves me so much that he gave his only son that I may be saved." Read your Bible, pray every day. Fellowship with godly and fruitful people and you will be fruitful. A bide in Christ. This is what our Lord says about those who abide in him: "I am the vine; you are the branches. If a man remains in me and I in him, he will bear much fruit, apart from me you can do nothing." John 15:5

---

[13] Matthew 27:32

Chapter Sixteen

THE HOLY TRINITY AND TRANSFORMATION

The story of Peter and Paul is that of continues transformation into the likeness of Christ. Peter's transformation started when he denied Jesus three time. He had earlier vow that "Lord I am ready to go with you to prison and to death."[14] Jesus being fully God and fully man predicted what Peter would do: "Before the roster crew, you will have been denied three time." When Jesus was being arrested, Peter denied Jesus three time. Peter was even scared by a servant girl. Who looked closely to him and said: "this man was with him." But Peter denied and said: ' woman I don't know him." When he was denying Jesus the third time the roster crewed and then Jesus looked at him. He then went out and wept bitterly.[15]

The different between Judas and Peter is that Peter repented of his sin. The Bible tells us: "If we repent of our sin, God is

---

[14] Luke 22:31-34 focus on verse 33
[15] Luke 22:54-62

faithful and just and will forgive us our sin and cleanse us from all unrighteous."¹⁶ In my case, I committed great sin that Peter.

During the war of independence in Kenya, the British divided the Kikuyu into two groups. Those who sided with the British were called home guard. The worst were Mau Mau. They issued an order of forced confession of all the adults who were not home guard. My dad had died a few years before the emergency. The episode which made me angry was when our mom was taken for interrogation. She was beaten and her thump was broken. I still remember Gideon and I meeting with mom as she was walking home crying with the little food which my sister Jael had prepared for her. When I saw her crying, I looked at the sky and cursed God: "You call yourself Great Provider (Kikuyu name for God). Is this what you have provided us?" My brother Gideon (who was eight years) who was then very hungry took the little food and ate. Like Peter, on the 13th of July, 1958, I attended Revival Fellowship which met at the house of Harriet Evans. I repented of this great sin and God graciously forgive me and cleansed me from all unrighteousness. Since then, I have experience God as the Great Provider. Thank you, Father, for forgiving me my sin and for even protecting me and my family.

After the resurrection, Peter has to face the risen Lord who asked him "Simon son of John, do you truly love me more than these." "Yes Lord", he said,

"You know that I love you". The Jesus said: "feed my lambs." When Peter was asked the third time he was hurt and responded: "Lord you know all things and you know that I love you."¹⁷ Here, the Holy Trinity was transforming Peter who had "a better than thou" attitude. However, Peter thought that he was called to preach to the Jews only. He has to face another three when he was being prepared to reach out to Cornelius who was gentile.

[16] I John 1:9
[17] John 21:15-17

The Holy Trinity had prepared this gentile who, when he was praying at **three** in the afternoon an angel appeared to him. The very time Cornelius was praying Peter was staying Simon, the tanner. Note that it was against the Law of Moses for the devout Jew to stay with a tanner. But now Peter is breaking cultural barriers! Note the **three** in the story of Peter as he was being prepared to reach out someone of a different nation. He went on the roof to pray and while he was praying, he fell into a trance. He saw heaven opened and something like a large sheet being let down to the earth by its four corners. In Jewish symbolism four is the image of cosmos. The sheet had **three** categories of animals- four footed animals, reptiles and birds. Peter was told to do **three things**: 1 Get up. 2. Kill 3. Eat. He refused and said: "I have never eaten anything impure. The voice said, "Do not call anything impure that God has made clean." Then the Bible says: "This happened **three times.** When he was still pondering the vision, the Spirit said to him: **three men** are waiting for you.

Arriving at Cornelius, he was welcomed with lot of humility. He found a large number of the gentiles waiting for him. He began the message by preaching to himself: "You are well aware that it is against the law for a Jew to associate with a gentile or visit him. But God has shown me that I should not call anyone impure or unclean. So, when I was sent for, I came without raising any objection. May I ask why you sent for me? Then Cornelius informed Peter how the angel appeared to him and told him to invite Peter. When Peter was preaching, the Holy Spirit came on all who heard the message. This was a great surprise for the Jews who had come with Peter.[18]

When the word reached Jerusalem that Peter has visited the Gentiles and won them for Christ, the circumcised believers criticized him and said: "you went into the house of unsurmised men and eat with them."[19] Note that the complainers did not refer to Cornelius as a human being. He was uncircumcised.

[18] Acts Chapter 10
[19] Acts 11:3

However, Peter explained fully about the vision and what he did. He then concluded: "So if God gave them the same gift as he gave us, who believe in the Lord Jesus Christ, who I am to think that I could oppose God? And when they heard this, they had no farther objection."

I can fully understand where Jerusalem Jews were coming from because. I am a black Jew of Kenya and circumcision is very important to my tribe. Our people are the largest tribe followed by Lou (President Obama's tribe). There was enmity between the two tribes. A Kikuyu talked about the Luo in a very negative way: "When you find it knock it on the head for it is a western animal". The Luo's will say: "the only good Kikuyu is only the one in the grave." Motivated by this hate in 2007, these tribes killed each other. One of the methods the kikuyu used was uprooting the whole sexual organ of a Luo. I praise the Holy Trinity for his intervention. It started with Luo religious elders visiting with their political leader, Raila and asks him to go and reconcile with Uhuru Kenyatta, the President of Kenya. And the Kikuyu Bishops went and convinced Uhuru to reconcile with Raila. When the two met, they stayed for a while staring at each other without knowing what to say. But graciously they reconciled and shook hands publicly. They started what is called building the bridge initiative (BPI) which has ended enmity between the two tribes. This was the work of the Holy Trinity.

One of the greatest blessing that Mary and I have was that our pastors and mentors where from different tribes and nations. One of this was a Luo by the name Peter Owit who we nickname Peter the Rock. He was Spirit filled and used to walk like a lion. He preached the Gospel everywhere including in beer hall. It was from him that I learned to preach the Gospel everywhere when I was a teenager in Nakuru. We were also having weekly fellowship which included all tribes and denominations except Roman Catholic. It is this seed which help us to reach out to all nations.

Interestingly ANCCI University students and alumni include the Roman Catholic. We have learned to forgive, to love all people and to draw from their unique heritages so as to enrich our lives and become more productive. From our Catholic students I learn to have daily reflection of the Saint. They gave me *ALL SAINTS: Daily Reflections on Saints, Prophets and Witness for Our Time* by Robert Ellsberg. I hope you will not laugh at me when I tell you that it was a Catholic Alumni who bought for me smart phone and taught me how to use Cash App and it was a Brazil daughter who taught me how to put the phone in flight mode. More about this in MINISTRY TO ALL NATIONS.

Another person who went through transformation is Paul. AS my beloved nephews Stephen Mbatia describes him: "He was AL Shaban." He was on the mission to Damascus, to arrest and kill Christian when the Risen Lord appeared to him. When he was knocked down by the Risen Lord, He was told to do three things: 1 get up.2 Go into the city. 3 You will be told what you must do. He was blinded by the light from heaven. Three things happen to him. For three days. 1. He didn't see. 2. He did not eat anything. 3. He didn't drink anything. Thus, the Holy Trinity was in total control of his life. Paul became one of the most successive missionaries, theologians and teachers. He wrote more books in the New Testament than any other person. After being transform in the likeness of Christ he advised us to be: 1. Encouragers. 2. Comforters. 3. To be in Christian fellowship. 4. To be tender hearted. 5. To be compassionate. 6. To be like minded. 7. Have unity. 8. To avoid selfish ambition. 9. In humiliated, to consider others better than yourself. 10. One should not consider only his own interest. We should learn from Jesus who though God, humbled himself to death. When we do that, we will be exulted with Christ. Philippian 2:1-11.The former Al-Shabaab who went through transformation and leaned how to trust advises us: "Rejoice in the Lord always…Do not be anxious about anything, but in everything with prayer and supplication, let you request be made known unto God and the peace of God which surpassed all understanding will keep you heart and mind in Christ Jesus our Lord."[20] St Paul puts in a nutshell a positive energy for those who are led by the Spirit: "the fruit of the Spirit is love, joy, peace, patience, kindness, gentleness, faithfulness, gentleness and selfcontrol. To attain this spiritual positive energy Paul advises to: "Rejoice in the Lord always, I will say it again: Rejoice.[21] Let your gentleness be evident to all. The Lord is near. Do not be anxious about anything, but in everything by prayer and supplication let your request be made known to God. And the peace of God which transcends all understanding will guard your heart and minds in Christ Jesus." Philippians 4:4-7. When we have the peace, which transcend all understanding what do we put in our heart and mind: In Paul's words we focus on: "Whatever is true, whatever is noble, whatever is right, whatever is pure, whatever is admirable, whatever is excellent and praiseworthy. Philippians 4:8

Transformed Peter also advises us: "Humble yourselves under God's might hand that he may lift you up in due time. "Casting all your anxiety on Him, because he cares for you." 1 Peter 5:6-7 David also add something for those who walk in Spirit and are being transformed:

"Delight yourself in the Lord;
And he will give you the desire of your heart.
Commit your ways to the Lord; trust in him and he will do this:
He will make your righteousness shine like the down,
The justice of your cause like the noonday sun." Psalm 37:4-5.

---

[20] Philippians 4:6-7
[21] Philippians 4:4

Chapter Seventeen

THE HOLY TRINITY AND AFRICAN PSYCHOLOGY

The first commandment command us: You shall have no other God before me. You shall not make yourself any idol in form of anything in heaven above or on earth beneath or in the water below, you shall not bow down to worship them." And the fourth commandment commands us: "honor your father and mother, so that you may live long in that land your God is giving you." Exodus 20: 3-4, 12. The bible tells us: " Children, obey your parents in the Lord, for this is right. Honor your father and mother-which is the first commandment with the promise: 'That it may go well you and that you may enjoy long life on the earth." Thus, God, father and mothers are the filters through which we received blessings hear on earth and heavenly blessing. In African psychology we have used the term the Tree of God for all that represent God-church, pastors, and the people of God. We have used Great Mother and Great Father represent the quality of motherhood and fatherhood. We will employ the insight from *INITIATION AND PASTORAL PSHYCHOLOGY: Toward African Personality Theory*. We will use Gikuyu mythology to discuss the three archetypes of the psyche.

A. The Tree of God

The name Gikuyu derives from Mukuyu tree. This is due to the fact that, according to myth of the tribe, Gikuyu who is the father of the tribe, emerged from the roots of the fig tree. Thus, the genesis of the Gikuyu people is associated with the tree. This tree will be termed the Tree of God.

The liminal entity included the rite under the tree whereby the senior adviser took beer and poured it around the tree, took some honey and smeared it onto it, and then prayed to Murungu, the ancestral God. He then took the milk juice from the tree and marked the male initiates on their cheeks, around the eyes, the center of their foreheads, hands, and legs. Then the wife of the senior adviser put the milk juice on both of the girls' temples, on their necks, on their nipples, and their hands. Symbolically, this rite connected the initiates with the Tree of God out of which Gikuyu, the father of the tribe came. Under the Tree of God, they were attached to the mystical sacred time when the Supreme Being was present on earth and mystically revealed himself, in human form, to the father of the tribe. They were also conjoined with other mystical beings, the ancestors and the cosmos.

Thus, the term Tree of God denote that which is in our inner world, which connects us with our primordial time, the Supreme Being, the mystical beings, the ancestors and the mysteries around us. It is also used for the external phenomenon, objects, insects, and animals that make us aware of this inner reality.

The Tree of God is located in man's "Garden of Eden." It comprises "the tree of the knowledge of good and evil" and "the tree of life," which sustains the human soul. It is the object and subject of people's myths, legends, sagas, proverbs, and idioms. It is the meeting point between humanity and the shekinah (the dwelling of God with his own). Under the Tree of God, we are made aware of the totality of our humanity and the presence of the God, who is the possessor of unique brightness and who-shines-in Holiness. It also makes us aware of the totality of our environment and our awareness of being and the complexity and the ambiguity of life. Like the ark of the covenant, the Tree of God has both healing and destructive powers (herem). In Genesis 3 we read about the tree that was in the middle of the garden of Eden and how our first mother and father disobeyed God and ate the fruit from the forbidden tree. We will now discuss the quality of motherhood and fatherhood using the terms Great Mother and Great Father.

GREAT MOTHER

The term great mother refers to the feminine quality which is predominant in women, but which is also found in a fully functioning male person. The archetypical motif of great mother is found in mythology and human history. She has both positive and negative aspects.

A. THE MYTH AND REALITY OF THE GREAT MOTHER

The Gikuyu myth includes two great women. The first one is Mumbi``, the mother of the tribe and wife of Gikuyu, who had nine daughters and no sons. The name Mumbi means the creator and the molder.

The other woman hero is Wangu wa Makeri, who, unlike Mumbi, is both a historical and a mythical figure. Mythically, Wangu was a very successful warrior and a judge. But when she was at the peak of her reign, she became arrogant and danced naked. This act provoked men's anger and consequently she was dethroned. This ended the woman's reign in Gikuyu land.

However, I interviewed several people in order to get historical facts about Wangu. According to James Makeri, the grandson of Wangu, the husband of Wangu, Makeri, was a very wealthy man. He had a big land, a large number of livestock, and men servants. He was also a man of great integrity. For these reasons he was respected by the Chief Justice Karuri wa Gakure. The former provided the latter with lodging on his way to Murang'a. Consequently, they became great friends and, thus, Karuri requested Makeri whether he would like to be made a chief. Makeri refused and said that he would rather take care for his wealth, but recommended Wangu to Karuri. He informed Karuri that Wangu was a woman of great integrity and had leadership quality. Thus, Wangu was made the Chief. Eventually Wangu gained respect and became famous for her leadership. She had a strong army, which fought and won many battles. However, she only fought those who refused to comply with Karuri. The songs were composed about her victory. These songs were also urging those people who had not submitted to her to surrender to her and to the senior chief.

Muchiri Makeri, the stepson of Wangu argued that what made Wangu famous was not the battles which she fought and won, but her work of reconciliation. She reconciled Karuri with many Gikuyu families. On the one hand she persuaded people to support the Senior Chief and on the other, she persuaded Karuri not to fight those who were not rebels and those who had surrendered. In most cases, it was Wangu who ended the war by her diplomatic way of persuasion and reconciliation.

In addition, Wangu's home was a house of refuge. If someone committed a crime such as murder and was chased by people in order to be arrested and be killed, if he could run and reach Wangu's home before he was caught, that man was safe. Hence, Wangu saved many people who could have been killed. Another activity that made Wangu famous was the saving of innocent children who were being thrown to the hyena. According to the Gikuyu custom, if a woman gave birth to twins, their mouths were filled with grass and they were thrown to the bush to be devoured by the hyena. If a mother with a baby who was less than one year old died, the baby and the body of the deceased were taken to the bush to be consumed by the hyena. So Wangu wa Makeri ventured a new mission of saving these children. She instructed her soldiers how to save these children. The men had to wrestle with the hyena in order to save a baby. All the babies who were rescued were brought to Wangu's home where they were cared for by her. Muchiri said, "My main duty when I was a boy was to feed those babies with milk." Here we can see that Wangu was a forerunner of various organizations and institutions in Kenya, which are caring for destitute children.

Furthermore, Wangu was one of the first African leaders to realize that the first missionaries in Gikuyu land had something that was beneficial to the country. She studied McGregor of Weithaga Mission, her neighbor and found that he had something useful to offer - education. Therefore, she took some of the orphans to him. She urged her people, particularly those who were poor, to take their children to the missionary school. She also reconciled the missionaries with the chief justice. When she was reaching death, Wangu became a Christian and was baptized.

According to those who witnessed the dance, Wangu never danced naked. She had four pieces: the inner soft leather that covered her private part, an apron that covered her upper part, the skirt (Muthuru), and a long garment that covered her from neck to ankle known as riba, which is a long ceremonial dress like a long overcoat. It was this ceremonial dress, which Wangu removed in order that she could dance freely. Normally, one could not dance with a ceremonial dress.

Thus, Wangu was famous, not because of dancing naked, but owing to her hospitality, love, ministry of reconciliation, and transforming of Gikuyu tradition. She had the qualities of the ideal Great Mother.

B. THE POSITIVITY OF THE GREAT MOTHER:

The Great Mother as an archetype creates and repairs human relationships. She helps us to reach out, to join, to get in touch with, and be involved in concrete feelings, things, and people. She does not allow us to hang in the air, but pushes us right into the middle of events and things. Instead of being detached she involves us and urges us to be a part of happenings. She attracts us to the mode of being and relatedness.

In addition, the Great Mother connects us with our tradition. It is this essence that draws us to our mother-land so that we may be connected with our roots. It magnetizes us by in-going rather than outgoing and then leads us to the dark womb in order that we may be reborn. By registering us, the Great Mother generates new intuitions, fantasies, images, and drives. When this precious work is taking place, the images of water, home, cooking pot, cave, ark, coffin, and mountain appear in our dreams and fantasies.

And as we have seen in the myth of the Gikuyu female chief, the archetype of the Great Mother allows us to be non-structured mararanja. The story that narrates that Wangu danced naked expresses this quality, which is inherent in human personality. This archetype allows us to be irrational, ecstatic, and no moralistic. Its dynamism pushes us outside of the self and sets us free from the tribal taboos. It was this dynamism that drove Wangu to a mission of saving the babies, which were thrown to the hyenas. Saving these innocent twins was against the social norm of the time. The same dynamism empowered great men like William Wilberforce and Abraham Lincoln in their war against slavery.

This quality of the Great Mother allows us to be emotionally involved, to take risks, and, thereby, enlarge our ego boundaries. It inspires us and fills us with vitality. It throws us to the forces, which are above and beyond our limitations.

The Great Mother is the source of life and nourishment. In her and through her, an individual is soothed, comforted, and cherished. Nyumba (the mother's house) in which she dwells is the theatre of riddles, stories, and jokes. In this dwelling, an individual is free to be what Urban T. Holmes termed as a receptive mode of human consciousness. This mode of consciousness as opposed to action mode, processes experience in spatial images, in concrete rather than abstract ways, in holistic or relational over analytical or differentiated modes, in nonlinear terms rather than linear, analogically and not digitally, and through intuitive thinking as opposed to rational thought.

GREAT FATHER

The term Great Father will refer to the male aspect of human nature, which is predominately in men, but also found in fully functioning woman. The archetypal motif of the Great Father is evident in myths, idioms, and proverbs.

Structure and emotionlessness, which are the attributes of the Great Father, were demonstrated and ritualized on the actual day of circumcision. As we have seen, even the girls were not supposed to show any fear or make any audible sign of emotion or even blink. During the summit of pain, she demonstrated fearlessness. She was expected to be highly structured. The male initiated was expected to show the same mannerism. All the initiates were challenged by the Great Father to be highly structured and to confront fear and pain with courage.

Since irua dominated an individual from birth to death, this quality of the Great Father reigned from childhood to death. I have always been astonished at this quality in one of my sisters. Mary who cared for me when I was a baby and a little boy. To my surprise, I have never seen her crying. Occasionally, when she was a little girl, my father would pinch her ear lobe and cause bleeding, but Mary never cried or even showed any emotion. She manifested the same bravely in defending me against any prey. One day, when we were herding, a boy who was bigger than Mary wanted to attack us, but Mary aimed at his forehead with a club, hit the boy, and knocked him down. I was amused the following day when the father of the boy came to report to my mother (this time my father had gone to glory) that Mary injured his son.

The other day, at age of sixty-eight, I reminded Mary of this incident. She bragged, "Even today, I am not yet old, and I do not allow anybody to step on my toes." This quality of life is typical to boys and girls who are unconsciously dominated by the actual day of circumcision. Since the archetype of the Great Father is within the collective unconscious, its quality is not limited to those who are initiated. It is inherent in uninitiated women as well. It is, indeed, found in all human families.

A. HIS DWELLING PLACES

The Great Father dwells in thingira (a traditional father's house). In thingira, one is challenged to be assertive and intentional. Here, mararanja dances are halted. The favorite proverb of the Great Father is, "Thiga has been circumcised, no more mararanja. " Meaning, since he is already circumcised, there is no more irrationality. This calls for economy of time and words. It also challenges an individual to be economically minded and precise.

While the Great Mother prefers stories, analogies, and metaphors, the Great Father favors a clear and logical language. The Great Mother entices us to be subjective. The Great Father urges us to be objective.

He enjoys sitting in parliament and in congress where he makes laws by which he governs and guides his children, in law courts where he judges and imprisons those who break the law, and in prison where he rehabilitates those whom he has imprisoned. Since the qualities of the great father are in both male and female, I do not, therefore, imply that the above institutions are or should be dominated by males. However, it is my argument that it is the qualities of the Great Father which are dominant in these institutions. To illustrates: During the staff institute of ATIEA, which I have already mentioned, I was in a team, which had to visit Arusha International Conference Center. After reaching this gigantic building, we were led to an office where we had to get someone who could take us around. Unfortunately, there was no one in the office. Consequently, we waited for several minutes. In the meantime, we were attracted by a chart on the wall, which included the pictures of all the government ministers. For those of us who were not Tanzanian, it took us as a surprise to note that the official title of the ministers is Ndugu (Brother). Interestingly, there were pictures of two women ministers whose titles were Ndugu. These were Ndugu Julie C. Manning, Waziri wa Sheria (Brother Julie C. Manning, the Minister of Law, and Ndugu Tabitha Siwale, Waziri wa Elimu ya Taifa (Brother Tabith Siwale, Minister for National Education. The use of the title Ndugu for a woman minister appeared to us as a contradiction in terms. However, our Tanzania friends informed us that the word Ndugu in this context meant a comrade. This was not convincing since the word Dada (Sister) could also convey the same meaning. Symbolically, I believe, the title Ndugu refers to the substance of the Great Father who makes laws and implement them in the government administration.

B. THE SUBSTANCE OF THE GREAT FATHER

Wisdom is another property of the Great Father. Interestingly, the Gikuyu ascribe all wise expressions, idioms, and proverbs to Gikuyu, the father of the tribe. For this reason, whenever a Gikuyu is using a proverb, he must credit the father of the tribe; it goes this way, "Gikuyu said, 'The day is for working, the night is for resting.'" It is as though the first father coined all the proverbs that guided the tribe in their daily living. The Great Father possesses the logos, which is the subtle fire emanating the whole universe.

This logos is characterized by fire or light. This light illumines and guides the human family.

Initiative, assertiveness, creativity, and objectivity are other traits of the Great Father. He challenges us to venture into new projects, to declare our standpoint, and to be ourselves. He admonishes us not to waste time with petty things. He challenges us to be and to allow others to be.... In this regard, the Gikuyu justify their individuality with a proverb, "One does not structure his family as that of his age mate." This meant that even though the age set underwent the same school, every person was an individual. For that reason, the Gikuyu discouraged over-identification. A person who aped another person was rebuked. If for instance, Mwangi noticed that Njoroge was over-identifying himself with Kamau, Mwangi would shout, "Kamau identification!" (Kamau Kanyi), meaning, you are not yourself but a false Kamau. Thus, the Great Father urges us to be ourselves. Thus, because you are wonderfully and fearfully made by the Holy Trinity, you must be yourself so as to use your unique gift for the community.

To be a productive person, you need a healthy Tree of God, Great mother, and the Great Father. The healthy tree of God is nurtured by accepting Christ as your personal savior. For he says: "I am the vine, you are the branchers, if the man remains in me and I in him, he will bear much fruits, apart from me you can do nothing." John 15:5. You much read your bible and pray every day in Spirit. You must be a part of the worshiping community. You need to discover the power of three. Paul had Luka, the beloved physician, Timothy and Titus. Jesus has Peter, James and John. He had Martha, Mary and Lazarus. You also need someone who is more mature than you who can be your Spiritual Director. And the spiritual director can also be your pastor.

You nurture you children by praying with them and reading the word of God together and encouraging them to attend children

Sunday School. As a pastor you need to have Sunday school, and Boys and Girls Brigade. Mary and I humbly praise the Holy Trinity for using us to start the first Company of the Boys and Girls Brigade in Kenya, which became the mother of the Brigade company in Anglican, Presbyterian and Methodist churches in Kenya. The organization gives as teen a mission statement, for boys the mission statement is: "sure and steadfast." For girls the mission statement is: "seek and follow Christ." More about planning the nurturing the Tree of God in all the development stages in *THE FRUITFUL FAMILY: Family Therapy Based on Christian Principles.*

To nurture the Great Mother and the Great Father, you have to honor and love your father and mother. As the Bible puts it: "children, obey your parents in the Lord for this is right: 'honor your father and mother- which is the first commandment with promise-' that it may go well with you and that you may enjoy long life on earth.'"

I humbly praise God for Mary because of her healthy Tree of God, Great Mother and Great Father. She is a father's daughter. Her dad regard her as a lucky bird. Being a very successful business man, he required Mary to see him first before he wakes up. She still remembers a day that she went to school and her dad come to school before he had to go and open the business because she had gone to school before visiting him. In my case, I am a mother's boy. As noted our community nicknamed her "Wagatungu" which means both the mother and the daughter of Gatungu. As we have mentioned, it was my maternal grandmother who first called me father. Being my mother's midwife, when I appeared, she reported to my father: "We have seen men and it is your father-in-law." As we were discussing our relation with the parents the other day, we remembered that we have one thing in common. I was never spank by my mother and Mary was never caned by the father. We also attended the church regularly since our childhood. The reward we have received from the Holy Trinity is that we are parents of many nations. My titles include, Abana(Arabic for Father), Padre, Patriarch, Papa, Father while Mary is referred to as Mama Mary, Madam, Nyina wa Andu(the mother of human being). We have indeed enjoyed each other for fifty-three years.

Nevertheless, the secrete of having a health Tree of God, Great Mother, and the Great father is by being in Christ. As Jesus said: "I am the vine, you are the branches. If a man remains in me and I in him, he will bear much fruits, apart from me you can do nothing." John 15:5. You will indeed bear the fruit of Spirit which is love, joy, peace, patience, kindness, goodness, faithfulness, gentleness and self-control. Galatians 5:22. That is all what you need to be fruitful and to attain a healthy human relationship

Chapter Eighteen

THE TREE OF GOD AND PASTORAL CARE

The Tree of God is so significant and that is why it occurs in both the first and the last book of the Bible. In Genesis the tree is placed in the center of the garden of Eden and is described as the tree of knowledge of good and evil. Adam was commanded not to eat its fruits. It therefore symbolizes the boundary line between what God allows us to do and not to do; what is ethical and unethical. In the Revelation, the tree of life is located at the river of the water of life which is following from the Father and the Son. Unlike the tree in Genesis, this tree of life is for the healing of the nations. It bears twelve crops of fruits and yield every month. It will be a reward for those who have washed their robes.

These people will be allowed to go through the gate into the city of God. These are those who were referred to by Jesus as wise virgins who had oil in their lamp, wheat as opposed to tears. Those who will not qualify to eat of the tree are: " those who practice magic arts, the sexual immorality, the murderers, the idolaters and everyone who love and practice falsehood." Revelation 22:15

In the Old Testament the tree of God is symbolized by the holy mountain-Mount Zion, the temple and the ark of covenant. The ark being the heart of the tree. Interestingly, the ark had three articles- manna, a piece of cloth of Aaron's robe and the book of the covenant.

In our time the heart of the Tree of God is the church, the Bible and the true minister of the Gospel. These will also include all those who are in and are led by the Holy Spirit. In the ark of the covenant there is power and spiritual nourishment.

I Samuel 3-7 narrate the importance of Ark and false and true ministers. Eli's children are faithless and immoral. Samuel is the true prophet. Interestingly the call of Samuel symbolizes a Trine God: "The Lord called Samuel three times and Samuel got up and went to Eli and said, 'here I am, you called me.'" Then Eli realized that the Lord was calling the boy. So, he told Samuel, 'Go and lie down and if he calls you, say 'speak, Lord, for your servant is listening.'" And when the Lord called the third time, Samuel said as he was advised by his Spiritual Director. And the Lord gave him the vision of his mission: "See, I am about to do something in Israel that will make the ears of everyone who here of it tingle. At that time, I will carry out against his family ...because of the sin he knew about; his sons made themselves contemptible and he failed to restrain them." Samuel was afraid to tell Eli what the Lord told him. But being a true prophet, he had no choice but tell Eli what the Lord had said.

I Samuel 4 -5 narrate how the Ark of the Lord was captured by the Philistines. These resulted to Israel defeat by the Philistines. But the Philistines experience calamity after calamity until they decided to return the Ark to Israel and then the Israelite gain the victory. This is a very profound message for those who persecute the true prophets. It doesn't end up well with them.

They will face the all-knowing and all-powerful Judge. As you have seen, the bishops, church elders who persecute the faithful servants of God incurred the judgment of God. As in the case of three Judases who fired a Baptist minister. One of them lost his job, the other suffered heart attached and the third one became blind and the pastor was called by a church which tripled his salary. So, if you are going through persecution for being a true prophet do not give up. Say with the Psalmist: "The Lord is my light and my salvation, whom shall I fear? The Lord is the stronghold of my life, of whom shall I be afraid?" Psalm 27:1

Chapter Nineteen

The Great Father and Pastral Care

In this chapter we will discuss the importance of the father in the family and the society. The Bible tells us that the father was first to be created and that he was created in the image of God. When God was creating all other things, he did it through the Word. The New Testament tells us "In the beginning was the word, and the word was with God and the word was God. He was with God in the beginning. Through him all things were made; without him nothing was made that has been made." John 1:1-3. But when it came to the creation of man, God said: "**Let us** make man in our image, in our likeness, and let them rule over the fish of the sea, and birds of the air, over the livestock, over all the earth and over all the creatures that moves along the earth." Genesis 1:26. So man was made through the union of the triune God. Not only that, he was made in the image of God, he was also made to rule over the creation. We have seen man having authority over the air and for that reason he can fly like a bird. He has power over the see and for that reason he invented ships which travel over the sea. Through the use of photonics and light and altering the speed of the light, he can send messages from one side of the universe to another within a second.

With this realization, how can we build up the father? The building of a father starts at birth. As I have mentioned, it was my grandmother who started the process in me. Being my mother's midwife, when I appeared, she reported to my father: "We have seen men, and it is your father-inlaw." My mother continued the process by calling me Baba(father) and the neighbors enforce this by calling my mother- Wagatungu (Gatungu being by given name this meant the mother of Gatungu and the daughter of Gatungu. Today I have many titles- Papa, Dad, Padre, Abuna and Patriarch. All these titles mean Father.

To have a healthy society we need to plant the seed of fatherhood in all developmental stages.(More about this in *FRUITFUL FAMILY*) . I must admit that I am so blessed by having a wife who has a very healthy Great Father. She has been building the father in me for 53 years. Besides calling me darling, and Rehema' father, she calls me The Father of the Human Beings (Ithe wa andu). As I shared at one time, I was staring at my office table with so many papers and I told Mary: "Come and see how your little husband is staring at the papers". She responded: "You are not a little husband. You are a gentle man and I love you." And then she gave me a hug. And my ego was strengthened." Mary's healthy Great Father was created by her father. She was her father's lucky bird. When she was a little girl, her father would not leave the bed before Mary came to the bedroom and then they greet one another. The father will say: "Wakiamaitu- She who belong to my mother. Mary then responded: Wakiawa- He who belong to my father. Mary has used what was imparted in her in our ministry in building the ego of a boy child and men.

To build the ego of a boy child, we have to consistently tell them that they are wonderfully made. We have to give them name which strengthen their ego. My father and mother-in-law selected special names for their children. They were named after great men and women in the Bible or prince and princes- They are Mary the mother of Jesus, Princes Ann and Jane, George(King George) and Samuel who was a great Judge, Priest and Prophet. The same with my parents they give us Biblical names. I have tremendously benefited from my name John which means: "God is gracious." Grace means getting something which you do not deserve. As my parents prophesied, I have received grace after grace.

On one occasion, when I was driving, I saw police flushing behind me. Immediately I remembered my name means God is gracious. So, I ask: "Officer, is there anything wrong?" Yes, responded the Officer: "You have two violations. You don't have inspection sticker and current road license." Is there any grace for me? I asked. " Yes." responded the officer. "If you have inspection today and get current road license and take the license to the police station you will be forgiven both violations. I did as he advised me and I was forgiven. We also had a police man who was our neighbor who volunteered to mow our yard regularly. The grace we have received from officers has influenced us to be making regular donation to police families and the wounded warriors.

Additionally, to influence children to honor the father, wives need to honor and love their husbands. This will influence the children to do the same. The husband also needs to love their wives as Christ loved the church.

Chapter Twenty

THE GREAT MOTHER AND PASTORAL CARE

The mother is as important as the father. The word of God puts it this way: "Children, obey your parent in the Lord, for that is right. 'Honor your father and mother- which is the first commandment with the promise- that it may go well with you and that you may enjoy long life on earth.'" Ephesians 6:1-2. The Bible tells us that the first mother was the most precious gift to man from the Creator. She was taken from the rim of man. And so, Adam said: "This is now the born of my bones and the flesh of my flesh; she shall be called woman." Thus, when a husband is honoring his wife, he is honoring himself. The Bible emphasize that: "For this reason a man will leave his father and mother and be united to his wife, and they shall become one flesh." Genesis 2:22-24.

To build a healthy family, the husband has to leave his father and mother and cleave to his wife and vice vasa. Both of them should not allow the members of their original families to come in between them. In marriage seminars that I led in Kenya, we found that the interference of the members of the family of origin was the one of the causes of problems in marriage. See *THE SECRETS OF SUCCESS IN MARRIAGE.*

To build up a healthy family, the husband has to love his wife as Christ loves the church. This entail building her up by appreciating her and training the children to respect and honor her. The words: "Thank you or you look nice," should be consistently flowing from the mouth of the father.

As we have seen, the special qualities of the Great Mother include imparting skills in human relationship. In my case, while I am my father's dream, it was my mother who trained me how to achieve the dream. She constantly told us that love is the law which bides all the law. She taught us to deal with each person the way he is.

The other important thing is putting the Holy Trinity at the center of your life. As I have mentioned, Mary and I start the day with prayer and reading the word of God. We also minister to each other. Our mission statement is: "By love, serve one another." When we face a great challenge, we use Mothers Union motto: "I can do all things through Christ who strengthens me." When worry knock at the door we knock it down with St. Peter's words: "Casting all your cares upon him for he cares for you." When fear is knocking at the door; we respond with the word of the Psalmist: "The Lord is my light and my salvation; whom shall I fear? The Lord is the stronghold of my life; of whom shall I be afraid? Psalm 27:1-2.

> The Grace of our Lord Jesus Christ.
> And the Love of God.
> And the fellowship of the Holy Spirit.
> Be with us now and forever more. Amen.

Chapter Twenty One

THE SERMON ON THE HOLY TRINITY

Genesis 1:1-30, Isaiah 6:1-8, Romans 8:12-17m John 3:17

Today is Trinity Sunday, on this Sunday we talk about God in term of Oneness in Threeness, so many illustrations have been used to illustrate this mystery. But none of them is adequate. We can talk about Oneness and the Threeness in the psyche. You have one psyche, but, according to Freud, the psyche consists of Id, Super ego and ego.

In a society or group of people there exists Oneness in Threeness. Talking about our church, we are one body but broadly speaking you can put us under three categories; Conservative (not in political sense) Innovators, and Radicals. Conservatives like us to retain things as they are. Innovators want us to retain the essentials in the tradition but innovate so as to make it relevant to the contemporary world. Radicals would like to demolish and lay a new foundation

The readings, including the Collect which forms raw material for the Doctrine Trinity.

GOSPEL

Today's Gospel lesson reminds us that the baptism must employ Trinitarian formula, "Baptizing them in the name of the Father, Son and the Holy Spirit. In other words, in baptism, we are conjoined to a body, which is indwelt by the Holy Trinity. Some current Christian apologists are describing the Trinity using the science of light/ Sherri Seligson identifies herself as a homeschool mom and the author of Apologia's Exploring Creation with Marine Biology high school curriculum, Interning for High School Credit and a few other books and media. She has noted an interesting model for understanding the Trinity. She observes that:[22] Light is an interesting study. It is comprised of three components. The first is visible light which is the colors of the rainbow, or white light. Visible light encompasses the light waves we can see with our eyes. You know when a light is on in the dark because you can see it.

A second component of light includes light waves we cannot see. In the spectrum of light there are ultraviolet waves, microwaves, x-rays. Those we cannot see, but we can see their effects. When you go to the dentist and get an x-ray on your teeth, you sit in a chair and they throw a heavy lead drape on you. That is to protect your body from the damaging effects of the x-rays. Those wavelengths of light are so strong, they can penetrate almost anything. We in our fragile human bodies cannot even stand to look at them or they would damage our eyes.

A third component of light is its giving of heat energy. If we're outside on a cool day, we want to stand in the sunlight instead of the shade. That's because the light from the sun creates heat. It is something we can feel but not see. Now think about this triad of light. Light we can see, light we cannot see but can certainly

---

[22] Sherri Seligson," God's Trinity and The Properties of Light" in Science and Apologetics on 07/11/14 at: http://sherriseligson.com/ gods-trinity-and-the-properties-of-light/

feel its power, and light energy we cannot see but can feel through its warmth.

With regard to the Holy Trinity, Jesus is the person who became visible to us. He stepped out of eternity to enter time for us, to be seen. It reminds me of the visible component of light. The heavenly Father cannot be seen, but we know of his immense power. We cannot behold him. He is too powerful. Sounds like the super potent wavelengths of light, right? And we know that the Holy Spirit cannot be seen but can be felt. Just like the heat energy from light.

Can you see how this creation of light gives us a glimpse of what a trinity can be? How three can be one? We cannot fully understand the godhead, but we can capture a greater understanding of that trinity when we learn more of the creation, during which time God made the greater light to govern the day and the lesser light to govern the night.

Pastor Robert L. McLaughlin of Grace Bible Church has a similar exposition on light and the Trinity. He proposes that, "light can also be regarded from the standpoint of its composition. Light is one substance, but it is composed of three different properties: actinic, luminiferous, and calorific."[23] He explains that Actinic light is a ray of light of short wavelengths that produces photochemical effects. Photochemical effects are related to the effects of light on chemical systems. Actinic light is neither seen nor felt, a perfect illustration of God the Father. Luminiferous light is light produced as a result of heat. Luminiferous light is both seen and felt, a perfect illustration of God the Son. Finally, Calorific light is light converted into heat. Calorific light is not seen but felt, a perfect illustration of God the Holy Spirit. In the end, Pastor McLaughlin notes that, "The composition of light is analogous to the three persons in the

---

[23] Robert L. McLaughlin, "Doctrine of the Trinity, on line in December 2017 at: https://gbible.org/ doctrines–post/doctrine-of-the-trinity/

Godhead who are one. Light is one with three properties. God is one in essence but three persons."[24]

The Epistle describes the substance of the Holy Trinity. "The grace of the Lord Jesus Christ, and the Love of God, the fellowship of the Holy Spirit be with you." The grace is accentuated in the Lord Jesus in that he gave himself to die for the people who did not merit the gift!

Love is accentuated by God the Father in that He demonstrated his love by giving his only son. John 3: 16 tells us, "For God so loved the world that He gave his only begotten son." Similarly, Romans 5: 8 teaches that, "For God shows his love towards us for while we were yet sinners Christ died for us." Fellowship is accentuated in the Holy Spirit; in that he is the being of God who dwells in us and binds us together.[25] Exhort us to praise, glorify and highly exalt the Holy Trinity:

Father, Son, and Holy Spirit.

In Genesis 1:1-30, there is delineation of singularity and plurality of the Supreme Being. This is particularly evident in the creation formula: *"And God Said:* "Let there be light, and there was light."[26] God said, *"Let us* make man in our own image."[27] "And so, God created man in his own image (in singularity and plurality), in the image of God he created him, male and female he created *them*."[26]

Subsequently, we were created by a being who is both singular and plural. And we were also created as "I" and "WE;" as Male and Female. Thus, life in its fullest is lived in singularity and plurality.

---

[24] *Id.*
[25] Canticle 13, Book of Common Prayer (Episcopal Church). [26] Genesis 1: 3. [27] Genesis 1:26
[26] Genesis 1:27

You have to be alone with God, so that you may know what to impart to the body of Christ. You have also to be in the body of Christ, so that you may draw from the body. We should also not lose the sight of the fact that we were created as male and female. This entails that we have to learn to live with persons of our own sex and the opposite sex. But more important we have to live with and in the Holy Trinity. This is why we conclude our prayers with grace as follows:

The grace of our Lord Jesus Christ,
And the Love of God,
And the fellowship of the Holy Spirit,
Be with us all. Amen

Chapter Twenty Two

ATHANASIAN CREED

The Athanasian Creed is named for Athanasius, a fourth-century bishop of Alexandria, Egypt, Africa, who was prominent defender of Trinitarianism. The creed, which has Latin origins, declares key beliefs about the Trinity, specifically, the equal nature of the three persons. It is one of three creeds accepted by major denominations including All Nations Christian Church International. It gives us the best definition of the God who has revealed himself as one in three.

ATHANASIAN CREED

Whosoever will be saved, before all things it is necessary that he hold the catholic faith. Which faith unless everyone does keep whole and undefiled, without doubt he shall perish everlastingly. And the catholic faith is this: that we worship one God in Trinity, and Trinity in Unity; neither confounding the Persons, nor dividing the essence. For there is one Person of the Father; another of the Son; and another of the Holy Ghost. But the Godhead of the Father, of the Son, and of the Holy Ghost, is all one; the Glory equal, the Majesty coeternal. Such as the Father is; such is the

Son; and such is the Holy Ghost. The Father uncreated; the Son uncreated; and the Holy Ghost uncreated. The Father unlimited; the Son unlimited; and the Holy Ghost unlimited. The Father eternal; the Son eternal; and the Holy Ghost eternal. And yet they are not three eternals; but one eternal. As also there are not three uncreated; nor three infinites, but one uncreated; and one infinite. So likewise, the Father is Almighty; the Son Almighty; and the Holy Ghost Almighty. And yet they are not three Almighties; but one Almighty. So, the Father is God; the Son is God; and the Holy Ghost is God.

And yet they are not three Gods; but one God. So likewise, the Father is Lord; the Son Lord; and the Holy Ghost Lord. And yet, not three Lords; but one Lord. For like as we are compelled by the Christian verity; to acknowledge every Person by himself to be God and Lord; So are we forbidden by the catholic religion; to say, there are three Gods, or three Lords. The Father is made of none; neither created, nor begotten. The Son is of the Father alone; not made, nor created; but begotten. The Holy Ghost is of the Father and of the Son; neither made, nor created, nor begotten; but proceeding. So, there is one Father, not three Fathers; one Son, not three Sons; one Holy Ghost, not three Holy Ghosts. And in this Trinity, none is before, or after another; none is greater, or less than another. But the whole three Persons are coeternal, and coequal. So that in all things, as aforesaid; the Unity in Trinity, and the Trinity in Unity, is to be worshipped. He therefore that will be saved, let him thus think of the Trinity

Furthermore, it is necessary to everlasting salvation; that he also believe faithfully the Incarnation of our Lord Jesus Christ. For the right Faith is, that we believe and confess; that our Lord Jesus Christ, the Son of God, is God and Man; God, of the Substance [Essence] of the Father; begotten before the worlds; and Man, of the Substance [Essence] of his mother, born in the world. Perfect God; and perfect Man, of a reasonable soul and human flesh subsisting.

Equal to the Father, as touching his Godhead; and inferior to the Father as touching his Manhood. Who although he is God and Man; yet he is not two, but one Christ. One; not by conversion of the Godhead into flesh; but by assumption of the Manhood into God. One altogether; not by confusion of Substance [Essence]; but by unity of Person. For as the reasonable soul and flesh is one man; so God and Man is one Christ; Who suffered for our salvation; descended into hell; rose again the third day from the dead. He ascended into heaven; he sitteth on the right hand of God the Father Almighty, from whence he will come to judge the living and the dead. At whose coming all men will rise again with their bodies; And shall give account for their own works. And they that have done good shall go into life everlasting; and they that have done evil, into everlasting fire. This is the catholic faith; which except a man believe truly and firmly, he cannot be saved.

www.ingramcontent.com/pod-product-compliance
Lightning Source LLC
LaVergne TN
LVHW020427080526
838202LV00055B/5068